Developmental Regionalism and the Political Economy of Africa's Integration

Developmental Regionalism and the Political Economy of Africa's Integration

Gabila Fohtung Nubong

LEXINGTON BOOKS
Lanham • Boulder • New York • London

Published by Lexington Books
An imprint of The Rowman & Littlefield Publishing Group, Inc.
4501 Forbes Boulevard, Suite 200, Lanham, Maryland 20706
www.rowman.com

86-90 Paul Street, London EC2A 4NE

British Library Cataloguing in Publication Information Available

Library of Congress Cataloging-in-Publication Data

Names: Nubong, Gabila, author.
Title: Developmental regionalism and the political economy of Africa's integration / Gabila Nubong.
Description: Lanham : Lexington Books, 2023. | Includes bibliographical references and index.
Identifiers: LCCN 2023000388 (print) | LCCN 2023000389 (ebook) | ISBN 9781793617392 (cloth) | ISBN 9781793617408 (ebook)
Subjects: LCSH: Economic development—Political aspects—Africa. | Regional economics—Africa. | Africa—Economic integration.
Classification: LCC HC800 .N8255 2023 (print) | LCC HC800 (ebook) | DDC 338.96—dc23/eng/20230110
LC record available at https://lccn.loc.gov/2023000388
LC ebook record available at https://lccn.loc.gov/2023000389

∞™ The paper used in this publication meets the minimum requirements of American National Standard for Information Sciences—Permanence of Paper for Printed Library Materials, ANSI/NISO Z39.48-1992.

Contents

Acknowledgements

I want to thank God for giving me the strength, wisdom, passion and inspiration to write on this subject. I want to acknowledge Jesus Christ as my personal Lord and Saviour; in Him I live, in Him I move and in Him I have my being.

I would like to acknowledge the support of my university, The North-West University, for creating a conducive environment and promoting a culture of research and innovation. Particularly my faculty under the leadership of my Executive Dean Prof. Babs Surujlal for his visionary leadership in promoting young and emerging scholars to pursue their research interests. I want to thank the leadership and my colleagues at the School of Economics for also creating a wonderful collegial work environment. I also want to acknowledge my academic mentors, Prof Lorenzo Fioramonti, and Prof Siphamandla Zondi under whose guidance, some of the ideas in this book were nurtured.

I want to recognise, appreciate and thank my wife Barbara Nubong CA(SA) for her wonderful love and support over the years of our being together and for being my number one fan and allowing me to pursue and grow my career from the base of a peaceful home environment. It took her diligence around the home to afford me the luxury of retreating to reflect and write. I want to also acknowledge my mother Mrs Fohtung Hortensia Ngang for her live long believe in me. She has been the coach behind the scenes that has brought out the man in me from the age of seven. I am grateful to my in-laws, particularly my mother-in-law, Mama Miriam Ayafor for giving me the best wife and Daddy Ebenezer Ndaya for being a wonderful father. They stepped in as a pillar of strength around which the family has grown after a series of turbulent years.

I salute the memory of my late father, Daniel Bobimwoh Fohtung, my late brother, Marc Etienne Forbah Fohtung, gone too soon; one with whom I will never have the privilege of aging together. He was the very early compass in my life who pointed me to my wife and to my career, the reason why I did History in secondary school instead of Human Biology. He taught me how to play the game of chess and table tennis; he was a real big brother in the real sense of the word. Furthermore, I wish to acknowledge the support of my other siblings and their spouses namely: Mrs Vivian and Apostle Edwin Mukong, Mr and Mrs Miriam and Aloysious Ayuk. In addition, I recognise the love and support of my in-laws namely: Dr (s) Ivan and Louisa Ndamukong, Pastor Emmanuel and Ruth Foyere, Dr(s) Amusa and Grace Ntatin and their children, all these years.

I dedicate this book to our children, Ezra Ian Bachangti Fohtung, Carla Seipime Nubong Fohtung and Charis Thandiwe Nubong Fohtung, who daily give Barbara and I a reason to become a better version of ourselves. This book is written with your generation and the generation of Africans after you in mind; those for whom a new re-imagined Africa will not be a distant impossibility but a reality.

Chapter 1

Why a Book on Developmental Regionalism?

INTRODUCTION

Although playing host to some of the world's fastest-growing economies in the last two decades African countries remain predominantly dependent on exports of primary products in the agricultural, mining and extractive industries. According to the 2022 UNCTAD Africa report, 45 African economies are commodity-dependent, which makes for highly volatile revenues due to the nature of the global commodity markets, characterised by periods of price boom and bust. This high concentration of exports in a small number of commodity products can create macroeconomic instability, especially during times of commodity price volatility and global shocks, such as those affecting supply and demand. Periods of commodity price booms on the other hand come with a surge in revenue for these commodity-dependent economies, which over the years have presented opportunities for African countries to diversify their economies and engage in productive processes with higher value addition and progression along global production value chains. The mixture of opportunities and challenges remains a reality for most African economies that still face considerable developmental challenges and host a number of debt-ridden fragile economies.

As the world attains higher levels of multipolarity with new partnerships and opportunities being created, is Africa ready to play a more active role in pursuing its developmental objectives, overcoming its common challenges and asserting itself as a major player in the new emerging realities of global geopolitics? From the look of things, there is currently great potential for African economies to transform and achieve a higher level of diversification and competitiveness. The successful implementation of the African Continental Free Trade Area (AFCFTA), a growing middle class, an emerging consumer market, the increased use of financial services and technology, and dynamic private entrepreneurs, can drive export diversification and sustainable economic growth in Africa (UNCTAD 2022).

Although the continent, like other parts of the world, is also affected by the 2020 COVID-19 pandemic and, in 2022, is dealing with the consequences of Russia–Ukraine war, it has shown some recovery that has been supported by improved global trade and, rising commodity prices. The 10% rebound in global trade in 2021 aided external demand for Africa's primary commodities, especially from its major trading partners (China, the Euro area, and the United States). The rise in global trade lifted commodity prices from 2020 levels, especially prices of energy and metals. Consequently, growth in net commodity exporters is estimated at 8.1% in 2021, reversing the losses of 2020, when real output fell by 1.0%. The sustained recovery has also reversed losses in real per capita GDP in 2020: per capita income grew by 4.4% in 2021 after contracting by 4.1% in 2020. So although talk of vulnerability and dependence on commodities remain a risk often associated with the continent, there have been opportunities coming to the continent through new resource discoveries, and these occasional surges in commodity prices. Would these surges in revenue for African countries translate to the effective upliftment of its people and what are some of the challenges the continent has to address to uplift itself and position itself as a significant player on the global stage?

This book has been written with the objective of making the argument that there are opportunities that are present for the current generation of Africans to take advantage of and pursue the transformation of the continent. The transformation we propose speaks specifically to the structural nature of its economies, its revisitation of the old debates of its industrialisation and leveraging the opportunities that lay ahead of it inherent to its practice of regional integration, with which it has been busy since the formation of the Organisation of African Unity (OAU), now the African Union. By proposing a revisitation of the old debates, this book makes an argument that the pursuit of a model of a regional corporation that integrates integration and development objectives together and coined as 'developmental regionalism', represents the approach to be adopted by African countries to transform their economies and move them up global production value chains with the beneficiation and transformation of its minerals and the diversification of its economies through other avenues of industrialisation that have now accompanied the unbundling of production processes and the increased servicification of manufacturing.

Speaking to the question of economic transformation and diversification of its economies, the UNCTAD 2022 Economic Development in Africa Report focuses on rethinking the Foundations of Export Diversification in Africa looking at the Catalytic Role of Business and Financial Services.

The report highlights the enormous potential of countries in the region to transform and achieve higher levels of diversification and competitiveness through services, in particular business and financial services. It draws on new avenues of enhanced growth in the services sector that can strengthen both the backward and forward participation of African countries in high-end global value chains. In this regard, the emphasis is placed on a vibrant private sector and catalytic financial services opportunities within the context of the AFCFTA, which focuses on liberalising the market to enhance intra-African trade and industrial development. So there are opportunities to be explored on the continent, and these opportunities did not begin today, for a variety of reasons, Africa had long turned around the page of the narrative that presented it as the Dark Continent, although it still has to deal with a significant number of challenges.

As far back as December of 2011, the *Economist* magazine published an article 'The Hopeful Continent: Africa Rising'. Therein they were making the argument that after decades of slow growth, Africa had turned a corner and now had a real chance of following in the footsteps of Asia. So after the 'lost' decades of the 1980s and 1990s (in which GDP was declining), economic growth in Africa has picked up. Between 2000 and 2014, annual GDP growth in Africa has been 4.6% on average (UNCTAD STAT 2015). These levels of growth have given rise to what has come to be known as the 'Africa rising' narrative, one that sought to capture what was perceived then as a turnaround in the growth experience of the continent, symbolised by a gradual move away from the many centuries of lost, minimal or no growth. UNECA (2016) provides five reasons that explain the Africa rising narrative. They attribute this to *improved levels of growth*, technological progress and access to ICT, *improved Human Development Indicators, improved health, reduced mortality, improved sanitation and better education, a return to more peace and stability* on the continent, a significant drop in the level of violence, *improved economic conditions* as a result of widespread prudential macroeconomic policy management and fiscal discipline, improved business environment in some countries, improvements in trade performance and the creation of an FDI-friendly investment climate and business environment (UNECA 2016). While all these factors are mutually reinforcing and as important, the higher levels of economic growth often feature as the preferred indicator of a rising Africa, probably because of the impact it has on the other factors. The witnessed unprecedented economic growth rates have been fuelled by internal consumption, the prolonged boom in primary commodity prices and demand, accompanied by prudent macroeconomic policies and strategies.

When compared to some of the 'dark continent' narratives of the 1970s and the 1980s, there is an increasing air of optimism about the future of Africa as a continent. Besides a burgeoning youthful population that is fast growing into a vibrant African middle class, general levels of education, health and life expectancy are better today than they were some 40 to 50 years ago. There are more democratic transitions of government, more frequently organised democratic elections, and by far a better informed and better-educated citizenry. Some of these improvements, especially in the governance and economic parameters, could be attributed to the action of the continent's regional integration institutions like the African Union (formerly known as the Organisation for African Unity [OAU founded]) that, for example, made it a policy to not recognise any unconstitutional change of governments in Africa. The African Union, together with its Regional Economic Communities (RECs) have also been quite instrumental in the advancement of the market integration agenda on the continent, which has had as an overall objective to integrate the small economies of the continent with the objective of deriving economies of scale advantages of being integrated into the global economy.

Although there are some well-noted conceptual critiques of the market integration literature and its applicability for a heterogenous region like Africa, economic and market integration has remained and continues to be a cornerstone of Africa's economic integration agenda. From the Lagos Plan of Action (LPA) through to the Abuja Treaty creating the African Economic Community (AEC), there remains a consistent belief within the policy circles of the continent that Regional Economic Integration is good and important for Africa's growth and development including the economic transformation of its economies. From this premise, many ambitious market integration milestones and targets have been set and trade promotion objectives (like the drive to Boost Intra-African Trade (BIAT) pursued. One of the more recent pursuits in this regard has been the launching of the AFCFTA, which intends to transform all adhering countries into a common economic space with limited trade barriers between the participating countries and a large competitive market to attract global Foreign Direct Investment (FDI) and related multinational companies.

The principal reason Africa has pursued such ambitious market integration agendas is because of the developmental benefits that regional economic integration and market integration is expected to bring to the continent and its economies. In a sense, Africa has been pursuing inadvertently a regional integration model that was intended to achieve certain development objectives and developmental outcomes. In its pursuit, it has however limited itself to the much-taunted benefits of economic integration as often argued in the economic theoretical literature without a critical assessment of the ability of its economies to complete successful integration arrangements in the first place. Talk less of the conditions under which development could be secured through the pursuit of regional integration.

This was always assumed uncritically often sitting examples of successful integration arrangements around the world, whether from Asia, Europe or North America, ASEAN, the European Union (EU) and NAFTA, often served as examples of what Africa needed to be doing to be in conformity standards of the global trade and capital movement fraternity. This ought not to have been too much of a concern if the intended objective was only to encourage trade, by removing trade barriers and increasing the levels of intra-regional trade. An additional conceptual question is introduced in the case of Africa when one takes into account that the integrating countries are also pursuing development and the economic transformation of their countries and looking to integration as a means to the attainment of this objective. Unlike the EU, ASEAN and NAFTA that brings together all developed economies or a combination of developed and emerging economies and having to deal with far fewer countries (NAFTA which has been replaced by USMCA from 1 July 2020 is made up of only three countries, USA, Mexico and Canada) when compared to the African Union's 54 country integration arrangement. These highlight the uniqueness of Africa's integration trajectory and experience and partly justifies the relevance of this volume that intends to bring conceptual clarity to Africa's pursuit of the combined objective of integration and development, or development through integration which is increasingly being captured by the notion of 'developmental regionalism'.

Developmental regionalism simply defined would be cooperation among countries in a broader range of areas that go beyond trade liberalisation (or market integration) to include cooperation in areas like investment, research and development, as well as policies aimed at accelerating regional industrial development and regional infrastructure provision (UNCTAD 2013). According to Sloan (1971), 'developmental regionalism' refers to the joint policies of economic cooperation, coordination and integration among underdeveloped countries designed to accelerate the rate of development of both the Member States and the geographical region. So it is not completely a new concept in the integration literature, and there are signs that component of it is being advocated in the African Union's approach to regionalism; for example, there is a program of the African Union that is dubbed 'Advancing Industrial Development in Africa – AIDA', run out of the economic cluster of the African Union Commission, just as there is the Presidential Infrastructure Champions Initiative (PICI), another initiative of the African Union and NEPAD Development Agency, which as the name goes focuses on promoting the financing of regional infrastructure projects on the continent. These two notwithstanding the industrialisation and infrastructure promotion programs are not governed by 'binding' treaties' nor do they enjoy the same legal status as the Abuja Treaty for the creation of the African Economic Community (AEC). It seems logical therefore to make the argument that although the African Union integration process has evolved to include elements of developmental regionalism, it is arguably not effectively pursuing a developmental regionalism approach to integration because it is not giving as much push and impetus to developmental components of the regionalism project as it is giving to the market integration components.

This volume's contribution is to make a case for why Africa's regional integration pursuits should adopt a developmental regionalism paradigm. It begins by examining some of the concepts that have been alternatively utilised to understand regional integration. Chapter 1 lays the foundation and context of the book by making a case for why there is a need at this time for a book on developmental regionalism and the political economy of Africa's integration. It essentially makes the argument that because the practice of regional integration on the continent for the last 50 years has not delivered the kind of results and development outcomes that could have been expected, there is a need to interrogate the practice of regional integration on the continent from both a conceptual basis and taking into account the unique historical context of Africa's integration. Chapter 2 builds upon this narrative by briefly examining Africa's history and trajectory of integration and identifying some of the common challenges that it has faced with the implementation of its integration objectives. These challenges point to both a capacity constraint issue as well as the structural limitations of integrating African economies. Chapter 3 examines the key milestones and treaties that have thus far guided Africa's political and economic integration as a means of explaining why the attainment of certain developmental outcomes has proven to be challenging. The challenges with attaining the developmental outcomes of Africa's integration constitute the major basis for why this volume is recommending an imperative change of paradigm in Africa's approach and practice of integration. To make this paradigm shift fit into the context of other relatively more successful integration experiences around the world, chapter 4 briefly presents a comparison of Europe's and Africa's experiences of regional integration and the setup and functioning of their institutions of integration. Chapter 5 builds upon these ensuing chapters to make a case for the adoption of a developmental regionalism paradigm in Africa's approach to integration, while chapter 6 attempts to apply this developmental regionalism paradigm to a practical development question of concern on the African continent, which is the question of industrialisation. However, before delving into the above-mentioned chapters as outlined, the rest of this chapter shall revisit and briefly present some of the concepts of regionalism, regionalisation and regional integration as shall be alternatively explored in the rest of this volume.

CONCEPTUALISING REGIONALISM AND REGIONAL INTEGRATION

Joseph Nye has provided one of the most traditional definitions of a region as 'a limited number of states linked together by a geographical relationship and by a degree of mutual interdependence' (Nye 1965: vii). Although such a definition satisfies most conventional approaches to the study of regionalism, its focus on territorial continuity and state-centric action is nowadays considered reductive, as regionalisation processes have grown more and more nuanced, with important roles played by non-state actors (such as transnational corporations and civil society organisations) (Schulz et al. 2001).

The debate about the definition of 'regions' has often been extended to the distinction of several notions that symbolise different patterns and degrees of regionalism. The broad term 'regionalism' has been used in the literature to cover a variety of distinct phenomena, which Hurrell (1995: 334) breaks down into five categories that are analytically distinct but collectively enrich the discourse around the theories and practices of contemporary regionalism. These distinctions have included the notions of regionalisation, regional awareness and identity, regional interstate cooperation, state-promoted regional economic integration and regional cohesion[1]. Regionalism in this context refers to cognitive or institutionalised (state-centric) projects, while regionalisation points to processes and to de facto outcomes. Regionalism refers to ideas or ideologies, programmes, policies and goals that seek to transform an identified social space into a regional project (Bach 2013: 92). Since regionalism postulates the implementation of a programme and the delineation of a strategy, it is often associated with institution-building or with the adoption of formal agreements. In the case of Africa, as has been witnessed in other instances, there have been elaborate institutions set up to accompany the integration objectives of Africa as primarily anchored and driven by the African Union Commission. Although in resource endowments and legal authority, these institutions may not enjoy the same resources endowment and legal authority to drive integration in Africa as they do in other parts of the world like say in the EU where there seems to be stronger legal distinctions and delegation of authority between the supranational regional institutions that are in most cases truly supranational, and the nation states that still retain national sovereign on some areas of cooperation while pursuing inter-governmental cooperation in other identified aspects of the regional integration.

Regionalism that broadly accommodates the experiences of different parts of the world accommodates extreme heterogeneity of configurations, ranging from those involving the material organisation of transfers of sovereignty (regional integration) to cognitive and ideational projects (associated with the invention of regions and construction of identities within existing states). At the onset of Africa's integration, for example, it could arguably be considered an ideational project for the creation of an all-African identity rooted in Pan-Africanist values. The appeal for this level of idealism was a reflection of the context of world politics at the time dominated by the fight to end European colonisation of Africa. However, these ideational conceptualisations of regionalism is a more constrained concept than regionalisation which focuses on the build-up of interactions which may or may not relate to an explicitly asserted or acknowledged formal regionalist project. This makes regionalisation a more encompassing notion than regionalism because it takes into account processes driven by other stakeholders besides the state (Bach 1999: 184).

Regionalism can thus proceed from ideas or ideologies, programmes, policies and goals that seek to transform an identified social space into a regional project. Regional integration on the other hand can proceed by means of formal regionalism arrangements and regionalisation outcomes. It is about states agreeing to live by common norms and values, the deepening of cooperation, the creation of common markets, the free movement of people in a region and ultimately the creation of a shared governance architecture with legislative and governance competencies over the region (Landsberg 2012: 5). European integration, for example, clearly encapsulates the pursuit of common norms and values, encapsulated by the creation of a liberal democratic space and shared norms of macroeconomic and fiscal policy management. These are some of the terms and conditions for conditional expansion of membership that guarantee that certain governance norms and human-rights culture is upheld by all would-be members of the intended common space. In the case of the EU, it is being done alongside the objectives of the deepening of cooperation and the creation of a common economic space, whereas not the same can be set for Africa's all 54 country-driven integration project which has not evolved in the same manner. As such, although the EU and African Union experiences both share certain components of regionalism and regional integration characteristics, they also incarnate significant differences that enrich the conceptualisation of regional integration. As such, regional integration thus factors in earlier definitions of regions that took into consideration elements like social cohesiveness (ethnicity, race language, religion, culture, history, consciousness of common heritage), economic cohesiveness (regime type, ideology) and organisational cohesiveness (the existence of formal regional institutions) (Hurrell 1995a: 333).

There are however other conceptualisations of regionalism and regional integration that have been advanced in other disciplines and following different school of thought. From a reflectivity's perspective, 'regions' have been described as 'constructs', which are defined by discursive interactions at the political, economic and social level (Langenhove 2012). As such, regions are not predefined: they are subject to change over time, in line with the prevailing political, economic and social discourse taking place in each society (Acharya 2009). For example, the establishment of the European Coal and Steel Community (ECSC) was a response to German expansionists tendencies that led to World War I and II. This institution later became the foundation stone for the establishment of the EU which started off as an initiative to pool and share a common resource that had posed a security threat to the region. So to prevent the outbreak of future wars, it was important to bring essential components like coal and steel that fuelled the war under a common control and management arrangement. Just as in a similar vein the OAU that later became the African Union was formed in the 1960s to lead the fight for the complete decolonisation of the continent. Two different political motivations gave birth to regional integration projects in both continents, but as both projects evolved, they increasingly share more similarities in the setup of their institutions and the pursuit of their integration agenda and objectives. There could therefore be a broad range of factors that may be implicated in the growth of any regionalism (formation of regions) project, this may include economic, social, political, cultural and historical dimensions as the main considerations and key drivers of the integration project. As Hurrell (1995b) has argued, contemporary research reminds us that there are no 'natural' regions and definitions of 'region' and that indicators of 'regionness' may vary according to the particular problem or question under investigation. Some of these differences constitute the most significant disagreements between proponents of traditional regional integration theory (often dubbed as 'old regionalism') and advocates of 'new regionalism' (Hettne 2005).

Notwithstanding the above-mentioned conceptual nuances, there are certain definitions of regional integration that are more prominent in certain subject areas like economics or political science and international relations. In this regard, Ernst Haas the founder of the neofunctionalist approach, defines regional integration as the process whereby political actors in several distinct national settings are persuaded to shift their loyalties, expectations and political activities to a new centre, whose institutions possess or demand jurisdiction over pre-existing national states. The end result is a new political community, superimposed over the pre-existing ones (Haas 1958: 16). Seen from this perspective, regional integration is the process of transferring loyalty, expectations and decision-making power to a new, regional centre. This is in contrast with Karl Deutsch who defines regional integration not as a process but rather as a state of affairs: 'a relationship among units in which they are mutually interdependent and jointly produce system properties which they would separately lack' (Deutsch 1968: 192). This represents your standard agglomeration or economies of scale argument in favour of cooperation. This is also aligned with the early formalisations of regionalism introduced in the 1950s to1960s by political economists like Viner (1950) and Balassa (1961). They viewed integration as a gradual process of economic cooperation following inherent linearity in five concrete steps, beginning with the formation of a Free Trade Area (FTA), proceeding to a customs union, a common market, an economic union and a political union (Balassa 1961). Their definition has emerged to be the prominent conceptualisation of market integration within the economic theoretical literature. It has become so dominant that economic integration or market integration is commonly treated simply as regional integration. Although from all the different conceptualised and nuanced definitions of regionalism and regional integration presented thus far, this is clearly reductionist and unrepresentative. There are clearly different incentives, motivations and drivers of integration that suit more certain definitions of integration than others, but no single claim to a unique definition could be considered wide and broad enough to conceptually capture all the important ingredients and components of both the concept and practice of integration. While some definitions may emphasise the role of certain actors, others emphasise motivations while others focus on origins and still others emphasise predesignated or actual outcomes. All however contain certain elements of cooperation and collective action across national boundaries.

Cooperation and integration are deeply connected in the process of regionalisation. As mainstreamed mostly within the political-science literature, the pursuit of cooperation amongst states may have as an objective the ultimate formation of a certain kind of polity like a political union. Political cooperation often involves mutual policy arrangements among Member States aimed at attaining common interests and objectives. Unlike a political union or federation, political cooperation does not necessarily require surrendering one's jurisdiction to the central unit. While political cooperation amongst states may set out to ensure peaceful coexistence, friendship and solidarity, as well as mutual respect for national sovereignty, political integration towards the setting up of a federation or union may involve issues like the establishment of collective institutions, and the development and implementation of common defence or foreign policy (Biswaro 2011: 72).

Furthermore, the concepts of economic and political integration tend to be sometimes used generically and referred to just as regional integration without any express emphasis being made to distinguish whether a particular regional integration arrangement is primarily the pursuit of economic or political integration as they sometimes go together and often lead to the creation of similar or identical institutions. There is also often no clear-cut delineating line in practise to determine at what point an economic cooperation or integration project gives way to becoming a political cooperation and integration project as these objectives are often pursued congruently. This is particularly evident in the context of African integration wherein the formation of the OAU in the 1960s carried a very political cooperation identity and objective, to coordinate the decolonisation of Africa and champion the fight against apartheid in Southern Africa. It saw the creation of certain institutions that later on morphed into the managers of the economic integration agenda, once that was introduced into the agenda of the OAU in the 1980s and 1990s after the adoption of the LPA and Abuja treaties. This makes the African Union-led integration experience to be one that started as a political process, went on to take on an economic integration objective and is currently actively including developmental programs in outlook, all still under the auspices of the African Union and its RECs.

However, the objectives that cooperation parties set for themselves often point to whether or not their main focus shall be on economic or political cooperation or some combination of the two. In our study, we will make use of the term 'regional integration and cooperation' with the understanding that it contains elements of both economic and political cooperation and aims at the eventual creation of an economically and politically integrated region. Indeed, the conceptualisation, definition and delineation of regional integration and regionalism, including the variants that derive from the root concepts that speak to how and why regions are formed, including how they identify and pursue their objectives should leave one with the only conclusion that it requires some degree of flexibility and dynamism in approaching the subject of regional integration. If it acccepted that the definition of regionalism and regional integration can be versatile, then Africa's trajectory and experience of integration can be considered as an unfolding experiment that can eventually to accommodate the concept of developmental regionalism. A case is still to be made that Africa's integration is unique to its experience and history and has not been sufficiently theorised and documented enough to enable it to make its contribution to the tapestry of the rich regional integration discourse. Making a case for its adoption of a developmental regionalism conceptualisation framework could become an important building block towards the process of understanding Africa's integration experience differently and the extent to which it aides our understanding of regional integration experiences from around the world. This is the thrust and objective of this volume, which should extend to adoption of a different way of looking at Africa and its experiences in integration and development.

CONCLUSION

In the onset of the writing of this volume, the desire has been to offer a text that principally answers the question: 'What does Africa need to do differently about regional integration?' in the next couple of years and decades in order to guarantee a different development outcome for its people than what it is known to have experienced up to this point. There has been a lot written about Africa, Africa's development and Africa's future and our desire has not been to regurgitate some of this material that in our view though factually accurate has tended to only identify the obvious suspects and elements responsible for the (under)development outcomes of the continent. Typical issues and usual suspects often cited, like poor or bad governance, weak institutions, corruption and nepotism and the associated poor socioeconomic and human development indicators that are often tagged along with these discussions. However, very few people will argue with the fact that Africa remains a continent with huge potential and a lot of promise. Not only does it have the demographic advantage of a young and upcoming middle-class population that will make up a significant proportion of the global consumption class in the near future, but it also continues to enjoy rich endowment of resources (especially mineral resources with some more resources being discovered regularly and newer countries joining the list of resources endowed and rich countries) and resilience to harsh circumstances and hardship.

Optimism about the future of Africa is not enough because the future that Africa and Africans desire for themselves will not occur accidentally but will have to be the fruit of deliberate concerted efforts to do things differently, change course and place the continent on the right path to growth and development. Often at times when one talks of Africa, we may tend to forget in our analysis that reference is being made to 54 countries sharing a common geographical space, locked in by two major oceans, which may communicate some semblance of internal coherence and brings together a billion plus people into institutional and legal country arrangements that are full of internal contradictions. There is a lot of work that has to be done to make these 54 countries be functional and deliver upon their national mandates and imperatives to their people, nations and flags to whom they owe allegiance and whose resources their governments and leaders manage and from whence they derive legitimacy.

Given the volume of extensive research that there is already about Africa, its economies, their development and the progress of the integration agenda, one would immediately want to know what fresh new angle another volume on Africa would be bringing, and what new thing would such a volume add to the existing debates as they stand. From an economic development perspective, it is important to state upfront that there are two developmental questions being thought of in this volume, which are related in a sense. In the first instance, the question of the economic development of African economies is silent and predominant objective being pursued, while the means of the attainment of this is being assumed to pass by the vehicle of regional economic integration. With regional economic integration as the core argument of the means to economic upliftment of the continent, the focus unfortunately does not zero into the structural weaknesses and fragilities of the integrating economies and their inert abilities to attain development. It is therefore assumed, probably erroneously so, that the market size argument of integrating microscopic economies into large economic spaces would make them to be more viable entities to pursue both their integration into the world economy and derive the developmental benefits from market integration. In any case, a contribution to the debate on doing integration better should be a welcome addition to the discourse on Africa's development.

NOTE

1. See Andrew Hurrell (1995a), 'Explaining the resurgence of Regionalism in world politics' for an in-depth discussion on varieties of regionalism.

Chapter 2

The History of Africa's Integration and Common Challenges

INTRODUCTION

For Africa, regional cooperation and integration was pursued out of a desire for unity among countries that had just gained their independence from European colonisation. Ghana's first president, Kwame Nkrumah, explained the need for African integration and unity with the following words:

> I can see no security for African states unless African leaders, like ourselves, have realized beyond all doubt that salvation for Africa lies in unity . . . for in unity lies strength and as I see it, African states must unite or sell themselves out to imperialist and colonial exploiters for a mess of pottage, or disintegrate individually. (Nkrumah 1963: 145)

Nkrumah and the founding fathers of African unity firmly believed that a united Africa stood a better chance at influencing the course of its development and the nature of its engagement with the rest of the world. They argued that if Africa's multiple resources were used for its own development, the continent would be among the most modernised in the world (Nkrumah 1965: 2). The means by which Africa's resources would be used for its own development, given its unique colonial past, was therefore to come from unity, self-reliance and collective action. It could therefore be argued that promoting collective self-reliance provided the initial rationale for regional economic integration in Africa. As some authors have argued, the association of regional integration with transferring components of sovereignty, as occurred in Europe, to a supranational entity cuts across the grain of postcolonial African politics (Bach 1999: 181). Nkrumah as a promoter of African unity drew inspiration from the experiences of other regions in the world to advocate for a political union of African states with a centralised authority, which was to share certain competencies with the sovereign and independent African states. This could have been a very advanced form of political and economic integration, which would have probably seen all of Africa being run as a federation of autonomous states with a centralised political system and authority. Nkrumah argued in this regard that

> we have seen, in the example of the United States, how the dynamic elements within society understood the need for unity and fought their bitter civil war to maintain the political union that was threatened by the reactionary forces. We have also seen in the example of the Soviet Union, how the forging of continental unity along with the retention of national sovereignty by the federal states, has achieved a dynamism that has lifted a most backward society into a most powerful unit within a remarkably short space of time. From the examples before us, in Europe and the United States of America, it is therefore patent that we in Africa have the resources, present and potential, for creating the kind of society that we are anxious to build. . . . I know that when we speak of political union, our critics are quick to observe an attempt to impose leadership and to abrogate sovereignty. But we have seen, from the many examples of union put forward, that equality of states is jealously guarded in every single constitution and that sovereignty is maintained. There are differences in the powers allotted to the central government and those retained by the states, as well as in the functions of the executive, legislature and judiciary. All of them have a common trade and economic policy. (Nkrumah 1963: 216)

Although Nkrumah's vision for the formation of a political union in a federated Africa was never adopted, his call for Africa's unity greatly influenced continental efforts in the pursuit of regionalism. The issues he put on the table then, regarding both the benefits of collective efforts in the pursuit of Africa's development and the creation and strengthening of a central authority overseeing a political union, are still as relevant today as they were in the 1960s. However, the failure to adopt the idea of a Political Union, meant that the newly independent states, who were still jealous of their newly acquired sovereignty and nationhood, opted to pursue national development first and then integration as a secondary objective, without much thought per se of which option (political union or independent sovereign states) would be most suited for Africa's collective development. This economic development question only became a topic in the 1980s, when the focus of the Organisation of African Unity (OAU), shifted from its 'liberation agenda' (freeing all of Africa from all forms of colonialism and Apartheid) to an economic agenda with the adoption of the Lagos Plan of Action and later on the Abuja Treaty for the formation of the African Economic Community.

However, more than five decades since the formation of the OAU, the pursuit of the ideals and benefits associated with a United Africa has proven to be a challenging exercise. Challenging because the initial idea of self-reliance, though romantic and fine-sounding, did not translate into a pursuit of the agenda for the formation of a political or economic union on the continent. The contrary would have seen the creation of supranational institutions endowed with both the resource and political mandate to pursue development and economic integration on behalf of the continent. The absence of the implementation of such a model of deliberate economic integration as a means to development meant that the pursuit of development through integration was only going to be a by-product of integration and not a deliberate policy intervention with deliberate and specific outcomes. As expected, this also influenced the way integration has been conducted on the continent and the way some of the institutions that promote regional integration have been set up to function. The pursuit of a political union in a federalist Africa could have meant empowering the centralised/federal authority with legal and constitutional powers to govern the continent as one Polity. Including, assumingly, the imperative for the coordination, conceptualisation and implementation of development plans, guided by an effective pooling and reallocation of resources to the various parts of the continent. Nkrumah's dream would have seen Africa operate like the United States of America in a federation with semi-autonomous states who retain certain competencies at their levels but were subject to the authority of the federal government in other aspects of national life.

The fact that Africa did not go down the route of the pursuit of a political union meant that although centralised institutions were created for the purposes of coordination, they never really adopted a supranational character because the participating Member States did not effectively transfer components of their sovereignty for these OAU-created institutions to be managed. In addition to this, the OAU and its institutions were constantly underfunded by African Member States although they benefited from the enormous generosity of the aid and donor community to keep them afloat. This generosity from sponsors outside of the continent further raise the concerns of who owns and runs Africa's integration agenda and greatly challenges the commitment of the African Member States to their stated goals of continental integration. Furthermore the absence of the creation of truly African-owned supranational institutions, meant that the ones that were created appeared to only act as clearing houses for inter-governmental cooperation in what could be considered as 'a uniquely African way of doing regional integration'.

This notwithstanding and probably related to the 'African way of doing integration', African leaders through the African Union (AU) and its institutions, continue to make a case for Africa's integration. This can, for example, be seen from the recent adoption of the Continental Free Trade Agreement (CFTA), which is an Africa-wide free-trade agreement (FTA) designed to boost intra-African trade and pave the way for the future establishment of a continental customs union. In bringing together all 54 African countries with a combined GDP of more than US $3.4 trillion, the CFTA is an ambitious project that will connect more than one billion people to a variety of cross-continental goods and services through enhanced trade facilitation and greater movement of people and investments. The CFTA intends amongst others to focus on addressing seven priority areas related to trade: policy, infrastructure, finance, information, market integration, boosting productivity and trade facilitation. The choice of these areas is a reflection and testimony of some of the challenges that have been common in Africa's integration, from which lessons have been derived and imputed into the design of these new-generation programs and plans. Although the pursuit of integration in Africa has often been riddled with many challenges, its leaders remain committed to its pursuit. This is mostly because, for Africa, economic integration is seen as an important step towards industrialisation, and the development of internal continental trade, which ultimately would lead to a reduction of her dependence and vulnerability to fluctuating overseas markets and the improvement of her position and influence on the global stage. This comes from the early postcolonial days of the formation of the OAU where integration was seen as a means of mobilising and maximising Africa's scarce resources of capital and skills and as a means of forging the way to unity both politically and economically (Asante 1997). To understand how Africa's approach to integration has evolved and particularly the pride of place that trade and economic integration is expected to play in the development of the continent, it is important to briefly examine the historical origins of Africa's practice of integration, as shall be briefly presented in the chapter that follows.

THE HISTORICAL CONTEXT OF AFRICA'S INTEGRATION

The desire to integrate African economies on a regional and ultimately continental basis has its roots in the Pan-African movement which aimed at the unification of African forces against imperialism and colonial domination, recognised as an essential component of strategies of economic decolonisation long before the attainment of political independence (Asante 1997: 32). The early actors of the Pan-Africanist movement (particularly Kwame Nkrumah) have been credited with the actions that led up to the formation of the OAU, which – as the predecessor of the AU – remains a central focal point around which analysis of Africa's integration efforts is routinely undertaken. It is consequently a useful endeavour to follow the chronology of events from the activities of the Pan-Africanist movement under the leadership of Kwame Nkrumah leading up to the formation of the OAU in order to get the background and context around which Africa's continental integration has evolved. This background and contexts paint an important picture of how the fight for the decolonisation of the continent and the end of apartheid in Southern Africa resulted in calls for greater African solidarity and unity for its progress and development.

Colonisation had not been a uniform experience for all African countries and though most post-independence African leaders expressed support for and belief in African unity, they sometimes differed on how the same should be attained. Some countries approached the subject of continental cooperation and integration by building on existing structures and frameworks (for example, monetary arrangements amongst former French colonies). This sometimes translated to divergent foreign policy stands on a number of burning issues on the continent as the newly independent African countries formed their political alliances to respond to a Cold War context and sometimes aligned with the foreign policy position of their former colonial masters. This is the context around which the OAU was born and the foundation for Africa's unity established. Some of the more significant events that occurred within the early years leading up to the formation of the OAU and the possible influence exerted on Africa's integration efforts are summarily presented in table 2.1.

This sequence of events leading up to the formation of the OAU highlights a number of interesting factors that have shaped the pursuit of Africa's integration agenda to date. As earlier argued and supported by the record of events presented in the table, the pursuit of integration and Africa's unity traces its ideological roots to the Pan-Africanist movement and the call for Africa to unite in the fight against colonial rule. Nkrumah (1963) articulated this call for unity and integration with the following words:

> Africa, it is frequently maintained is poor. Yet it is widely acknowledged that its potentials provide tremendous possibilities for the wealthy growth of the continent, already known to contain vast mineral and power resources. The economic weakness of the new African states has been inherited from the colonial background, which subordinated their development to the needs of the colonial powers. To reverse the position and bring Africa into the realm of highly productive modern nations, calls for a gigantic self-help programme. Such a programme can only be produced and implemented by integrated planning within an over-all policy decided by a continental authority.

By situating the call for African unity alongside the fight for decolonisation, Nkrumah was making a case that Africa could only emerge from its past of

Table 2.1 Significant Historical Events Leading up to the Birth of the OAU

Dates/Place	*Events/Delegates*	*Decisions/Discussions*
1945	Fifth Pan-African Congress.	Addressed the question of colonialism.
15th to 19th October 1945 Charlton Town Hall, Manchester	Delegates from Ghana, Nigeria, Sierra Leone, Malawi, S. Africa, Trinidad and Trade Unions like the West African Students Union (WASU). Ghana (Kwame Nkrumah, Ako Adjei) Nigeria. (Obafemi Awolowo, Jaja Wachukwu, Nnandi Azikiwe).	Emphasised speedy decolonisation of the African continent.
1958, 23rd November	Formation of the Ghana–Guinea Union.	Assumed will be the nucleus of West African Unity.
	Initiated by Dr Kwame Nkrumah and Sekou Toure of Guinea.	Guinea had decided to cut ties with France, with devastating economic consequences and Nkrumah decided to step in.
1959, 1st May	Conakry Joint Declaration.	Intention to broaden the basis of Union
	Independence and unity with one flag, one anthem and one motto	Make it the nucleus of Union of Independent states of Africa.
	Signed by Sekou Toure and Kwame Nkrumah	Members to surrender portions of their national sovereignty in the interest of the African community
15th to 22nd April 1958 Accra, Ghana	First Pan-African Conference on the African continent.	Self-determination of all African States as per 1945 Congress.
	Egypt, Sudan, Libya, Tunisia, Liberia, Morrocco and Ethopia.	Expressed support for Algerian Nationalists at war with French Colonialism.
		Instructed their UN reps in NY to coordinate on all matters affecting Africa.
		Symbol of Political Will Overcoming Religion and Sahara Dessert Divide.
19th July 1959	Saniquellie meeting and declaration	Decision to hold Special conference of All Independent African States in 1960
	Ghana, Guinea and Liberia	
	Formation of Associated States of Africa (ASA)	Non-independent states with a fixed date were also invited, to work out a charter which would achieve their ultimate goal of unity among independent African States.

June 1960, Addis Ababa	Second conference of Independent African States. Also attended by Nigeria, Cameroon, Somalia and Sudan	Debate on the form of African Unity, African Unity with political integration (led by Ghana and Guinea) and common platform to coordinate their efforts aimed at achievement of their common objectives (led by Nigeria and Liberia). Discussed developments in Congo-Leopoldville. Algerian War of Independence. Morroco's claim on Mauritania. French Nuclear tests in the Sahara.
October 1960 Abidjan, Ivory Coast	Abidjan summit of former French West Africa and Equatorial Africa. 12 states: Cameroon, Central African Republic, Chad, Congo, Benin, Gabon, Ivory Coast, Malagasy, Mauritania, Niger, Senegal and Malagasy. Former French West African and Equatorial countries	Also discussed: basis for future common action for cooperative development in their respective states.
December 1960 Brazzaville, Congo	Brazzaville Group alias Union of African and Malagasy States (UAMS) formed. Set up Commission to propose plan for economic cooperation and development. 12 states from Abidjan : Guinea was absent, have broken away from France as well as Mali has separated with Senegal over the dissolution of the Mali federation.	Supported French intention to hold referendum and roundtable to settle Algerian independence issue. Expressed support for President Joseph Kasavubu in his quarrel with the then Prime Minister Patrice Lumumba. Invited all African countries to rally behind Mauritania to gain access to the UN since independence from Morocco and veto by Soviet Union at the security council. Study and report on form of relationship to exist with EEC as well as international organisations of financial and economic character.
December 1960 – Five days after Brazzaville Meeting	Guinea Conakry Meeting. President Kwame Nkrumah, Sekou Toure and Modibo keita from Ghana, Guinea and Mali	Announce Union of three free states aimed at promoting a common economic and monetary policy. Criticised conclusions from Brazzaville meeting as likely to jeopardise African Unity and strengthen neocolonialism. Also condemned all forms of African regrouping based on the language of colonial powers.

(*continued*)

Table 2.1 (Continued)

Dates/Place	*Events/Delegates*	*Decisions/Discussions*
January 1961 Casablanca summit	Casablanca meeting convened by King Sidi Mohamed V of Morocco. Ghana, Guinea, Eygpt, Libya, Algeria and Congo and Mali	Condemned Gen De Gaulle's proposed referendum and roundtable conference on Algeria and expressed support to Algeria provisional government to gain independence. Expressed support for Prime Minister Lumumba and urged UN to use force to end Katangese secession. Described Mauritania as a Puppet State created by France from Southern Morocco and support Morocco's move to regain the country. Constituted Casablanca group with a radical outlook, addressing the same issues as Brazzaville Group but disagreeing on every conclusion from Brazzaville. Casablanca group advocated for Political Union with joint military High Command, whereas Brazzaville only interested in Basic Economic cooperation. Meeting committed itself to giving material and financial support to all nationalist movements fighting against colonialism. On African Unity Conference, encouraged efforts to establish an effective and efficient form of cooperation among African states in economic, social and cultural fields
8 May 1961 Monrovia Summit	Monrovia summit to attempt to reconcile Casablanca and Brazzaville divided and cosponsored by Ghana, Guinea, Ivory Coast, Senegal and Liberia though Ghana and Guinea pulled out in the last minute. Full Brazzaville Group + Nigeria, Somalia, Sierra Leone, Togo, Ethiopia, Libya, Tunisia and Liberia subsequently called the Monrovia group. Morocco refused to attend because of Mauritania	Endorsed the positions taken at the Brazzaville Summit on all the major issues. Outlined principles to govern relationship of African States including – non-interference in internal affairs. – respect for sovereignty of each state and inalienable right to existence. – promotion of cooperation based on tolerance, solidarity and good neighbourliness. Unity in aspirations and action from the point of view of African solidarity and political identity as against political integration of sovereign African States.

January 1962	Lagos Conference Boycotted by Casablanca Group over the non-involvement of Algerian Provisional government. Monrovia Group minus Libya and Tunisia plus Tanzania and DRC	Adoption of charter for formation of an Inter-African Malagasy State Organisation based on resolutions adopted in Monrovia
22nd to 26th May 1963	Addis Ababa Summit. 32 independent states from both Monrovia and Casablanca Groups	Creation of Organisation of African Unity, with a charter representing a compromise of both positions.

Source: Author's Compilation.

subjugation and develop its economies to be globally competitive through a common political authority. He was obviously influenced by his strongly socialist inclinations and appreciation for centralised planning, but his philosophy of 'strength in unity' has been a foundational consideration in Africa's continuous pursuit of integration.

Another important consideration from this historical account is the fact that Africa's colonial past and the fight for independence supplied the institutional and leadership foundation upon which the continental integration edifice was laid. The colonial administration in most countries endowed them with their first infrastructure and economic development projects, including agricultural estates that continue today to contribute towards the export earnings of some African countries.

The colonial administrators also often administered groups of countries together, which facilitated the pursuit of cooperation by these countries after their independence. The British colonial administration, for example, created common research institutions for Kenya, Tanzania and Uganda, as well as common transportation systems, laying the foundations for future economic cooperation leading up to the formation of the East African Community (EAC). Similarly, the French colonial administration managed its territories as 'French Equatorial and West Africa', which eventually led to the formation of a monetary union amongst these countries post-independence. These pre-existing colonial blocks tended to form the same ideological positions building up to the formation of the OAU and did not necessarily approach the process as a simple pursuit of Africa's unity. There is a lot said about this aspect, which has gone on to the functioning and effectiveness of today's AU and the policy positions it sometimes takes in global policy issues. The short version of the story is that in a Cold War era, a number of the Nationalist leaders (like Patrice Lumumba of the Congo or Roland Felix Moumie or UM Nyobe of Cameroon) that fought for the independence of their countries did not go on to become the post-independence leaders of their countries, as they were mostly replaced by other leaders that were more sympathetic to the neocolonial agenda of some of the former colonial powers in Africa. As such the Organisation for African Unity was a political compromise project that took into account the desires of so-called 'Monrovia' and 'Casablanca' groups. This division from the beginning fragilised the 'African Unity' project from its onset and predisposed the organisation to work along the lines of these fractured positions for long after the formation of the OAU.

This shaky beginning was also evident with the formation of some sub-regional organisations outside of the OAU. For example, the EAC that is today one of the AU's most successful Regional Economic Communities (REC), is made up of countries that used to be administered together under the British colonial empire and have institutional arrangements that can be traced back to their shared colonial experience of cooperation. This was particularly facilitated by the infrastructural linkages (especially rail) created under the colonial administration. In the case of West African integration, the West African Economic and Monetary Union (UEMOA in French) assembling a number of former French colonies in West Africa evolved to become a Custom and Monetary Union within the Economic Community of West African States (ECOWAS). A sort of integration arrangement (UEMOA) within another integration arrangement (ECOWAS) and often considered as more advanced due to its monetary integration which is clearly of colonial origin. In this instance, as has been argued in the case of EAC, the linkages that existed between these countries under colonial rule constituted a platform for the pursuit of cooperation and integration in their post-independence. This approach to continental integration through the pursuit of piecemeal sub-regional cooperation was at variance with the views of other African leaders like Kwame Nkrumah who advocated for a unified continent under a centralised authority. Nkrumah criticised attempts to promote sub-regional cooperation on the basis of language and previous cultural ties and saw this as an open door for the influence of neocolonialism. The vestiges of these 'colonial era' affiliations continue to be seen even in today's AU, with some of the divergent positions held by the 'Francophone block' and 'Anglophone block' within the Union on key policy issues, wherein one is often found to be supporting the policy positions of France on key foreign policy questions on the continent, a divide which was very evident during the post-electoral crisis in the Ivory Coast in the early 2000s.

A very significant element from the above historical account is the fact that African countries notwithstanding their desire for unity approached the subject of the continent's integration from a divided perspective. This division became evident as early as at the second conference of all independent African states that took place in Addis Ababa in 1960. At this conference, there were those in favour of pursuing African unity through a full political integration (led by Ghana and Guinea) and those who only wanted a common platform to coordinate their efforts and achieve their common objectives (led by Nigeria and Liberia). Those who believed in the need to proceed towards a full political integration before any advancement in the social and economic fields could be achieved came to be known as the Casablanca group (named after a meeting convened by King Mohamed V of Morocco in January 1961), while those who maintained that a slower institutional process, founded perhaps on subcontinental regional groupings, focusing on functional cooperation was better suited to promote Africa's integration were later known as the Monrovia group (name given to the group of countries that attended the Monrovia summit of May 1961) (Olivier 2010). The Casablanca group adopted a more radical stance on Africa's integration, pledging support to nationalist movements and advocating the creation of a political union with a joint military command.

The Monrovia summit in contrast adopted a more conservative stance on the principles that would govern the relationship between African states. They, for example, advocated for non-interference in the internal affairs of African states and the respect for the sovereignty of each state and their inalienable right to existence. This group encouraged the promotion of cooperation based on tolerance, solidarity and good neighbourliness. These two groups did not only disagree on the pace of integration but also had divergence of views on a number of crisis situations on the continent at the time (opinions were divided on the Congolesse Civil War, support for Patrice Lumumba against the Katangese secession, the independence of Mauritania from Morocco, the French nuclear test in the Sahara Dessert, the Algerian War of independence and perceived French interference in its former colonies). It was against this backdrop that a meeting was convened in Addis Ababa from the 22nd to the 26th of May 1963, attended by 32 independent African States to found the OAU with a charter that represented a compromise of the views of these two groups. This explains why the initial conditions set out for the continental integration project had to build into it elements that could be perceived as 'anti-integration'. A compromise solution had to be reached that guaranteed the non-interference in the internal affairs of other African states and the respect for sovereignty of each state and their inalienable right to existence. These intitial conditions included the promotion of cooperation based on tolerance, solidarity and good neighbourliness. It also included the pursuit of African unity in aspirations and from the point of view of African solidarity. The creation of a common political identity like a political Union through the political integration of sovereign African States was not expressly adopted as an objective from the beginning, althrough Kwame Nkrumah was an advocate of the creation of a 'United States of Africa' as a political integration project. This is the foundation upon which the pursuit of Africa's cooperation and integration was built. The peculiarity of Africa's approach to integration seen from this brief historical account, is the fact that regional cooperation and integration was undertaken at more or less the same period when most of these African countries were acquiring the status of nation states in the international system. The first African country to become independent was Ghana in 1958. Other African countries that formed the OAU also gained their independence in the 1960s. These newly independent countries went on to form the OAU before they had accumulated any meaningful experience in self-governance or in the building of governance institutions. So in 1963 most countries were still at the very early stages of the establishment of public service and could not boast of civil servants that could staff their public service to pursue their national development agendas with sufficient skill and capabilities. Such capacity constraints would have extended to the supranational institutions that would have been created as part of the formation of the

OAU like the secretariat of the OAU. Capacity constraints have not been the only challenge with Africa's integration project; there have been quite a few other challenges, some of which will be presented in the section that follows.

SOME OF THE CHALLENGES OF REGIONAL INTEGRATION IN AFRICA

The story of regionalisation on the African continent is one in which political rhetoric and commitment to regional integration have not always been matched by implementation reality, as some of the objectives and targets have not been met (Olivier 2010; Draper 2012). Vanheukelom (2016: 2) blames this 'implementation gap' between the promises and delivery of the AU commission on its mandate on its ever-expanding agenda amidst the constraint of limited resources, lack of leverage and the absence of political commitment from some of its key implementing partners. Akokpari (2008: 106) has identified 'structural bottlenecks' that militate against effective integration in Africa, these include;

- The problems posed by multiple memberships of states in various regional organisations.
- Low levels of intra-regional trade coupled with the continent's stronger trading relationships with partners external to Africa.
- The prevalence of weak institutions, debt and conflicts.
- The tension between the states and regional organisations with respect to the preservation of their national sovereignty.
- Concerns over the unequal distribution of the costs and benefits from integration among states
- And the dangers of pursuing economic and political integration simultaneously.

While these have been extensively documented as noted bottlenecks in Africa's integration process, it is not completely clear why these bottlenecks have persisted over many years notwithstanding the belief in the developmental benefits of integration for Africa. Their persistence perhaps suggests a fundamental problem with the conceptualisation and conduct of regional integration on the continent. This may be most evident from the continuous membership of AU Member States to different sub-regional economic and political arrangements (Dinka and Kennes 2007; Draper et al. 2007; UNECA 2006 and 2008). Multiple concurrent membership in different regional organisations prevents these states from being fully committing to the core objectives of these regional organisations. Furthermore, multiple membership therefore undermines the efficiency and effectiveness with which these regional formations can deliver upon their developmental mandate. In addition to this, membership in numerous regional integration arrangements exerts considerable material, financial and human resources pressures on states. Since these countries come from a region that is characterised by scarce resources and weak institutions, the simultaneous implementation of possibly conflicting or contradictory policies as part of their commitments to their different regional arrangements is likely to take a devastating toll on the participating countries (Akokpari 2008: 100).

The costs and consequences of multiple membership should be clearly evident to the countries that persist with such multiple arrangements, whose analysts read and are fully aware of these criticisms of multiple membership. A curious question therefore remains one of ascertaining why these African countries still persist in the pursuit of multiple membership regional integration arrangements. One possible explanation could be the geographical space continuity that places some countries in several regions at the same time. For example, a country like the Democratic Republic of Congo shares land borders with countries from Southern, Eastern and Central Africa. Geographical land borders suggest cross-border trade, which may have to be regulated or contained within certain regional trade arrangements, thus compelling the DRC to enter into more than one of such arrangements with the countries with whom it shares such borders, which configuration would not be the same for every participating country. So there could be strategic considerations, reasons and justifications regarding this question of multiple membership, which has just not been sufficiently researched and documented. This could be another instance in which African regionalism could contribute to the global discourse on the behaviour of nation states in their participation and membership in regional economic and trade arrangements. In the meantime, the AU has found other ways of addressing this question of multiple membership by pushing for rationalisation of the regional integration arrangements. It is for this reason that the AU is determined to recognise only eight of the many regional organisations that have been created on the continent. These are meant to serve as building blocks to continental integration.

The AU's model of using its RECs like ECOWAS, EAS and SADC is also another unique characteristic of its model of integration. This is because, unlike the experience in most other regions, these RECs do actually function and exercise influence within their regions on a range of issues related to safety and security or development for the cause of integration in ways in which not even the AU does. There seems to be some kind of subsidiarity in the distribution and execution of their functions, such that, for example, in the area of peace and security the regional economic community is often the one that takes the lead in addressing regional conflicts before the AU gets involved, if at all it does. This was the case of ECOWAS in the post-electoral crisis in Ivory Coast or in the more recent instance of SADC's intervention to resolve the security situation in the north of Mozambique. It should be noted that these RECs also have elaborate institutional arrangements and sets up for their region that are completely different and separate from those of the AU. So ECOWAS as a building block of the AU does not host a 'secretariat on behalf of or of the AU' in West Africa. ECOWAS like SADC and all the other RECs have just been adopted by the AU through a recognition process that seeks to attain coherence in the continental integration project, but these organisations are regional organisations in their own right, with a unique history, clearly defined institutions, leadership and mandate. They tend to be responsive to the economic and political challenges of their region, forge better bonds and ties within their region and quite often present a greater internal coherence than can sometimes be observed within the broader continental integration fraternity. This is what makes them the blocks of the AU, but not blocks that were deliberately created as part of a well-crafted, properly designed and implemented integration project. They are more blocks that became blocks because they are naturally part of a collective ongoing endeavour into which they naturally fit in.

With such a context and background, it can become understandably a challenging exercise to harmonise custom policies amongst the participating members that belong to a number of different regional economic integration arrangements at the same time as they are trying to fit into the whole continental agenda. Countries therefore choose which regional arrangement to belong to not based on a preoccupation with the impact of multiple membership on continental integration but based on which arrangement best serves their immediate strategic interest and developmental needs and aspirations. They consequently find themselves subscribing to multiple regional organisations to derive the benefits that each may have to offer. Seen from this perspective, multiple membership though costly and disadvantageous becomes justifiable in the eyes of the participating AU Member States when assessed through the lens of the pursuit of their strategic interests. It is arguably not healthy for continental integration (as some analysts love to argue within the 'spaghetti bowl' narrative) but there is certainly a logic to it. There are two important points worth making at this point. The first being that Africa's approach to integration thus far should really be perceived as an unfolding experiment whose lessons are still in the making as opposed to it being perceived as a failed or poorly implemented regional integration ideal that is different from what is happening elsewhere. Once seen and appreciated from this perspective, it will be possible to understand why certain things happen the way they are happening in Africa and in addition to this, what lessons can be learned from this uniquely African experience when compared to the experiences of the other parts of the world. The second point, which is related to one of the core objectives of this volume, is the call to rethink Africa's economic integration and its pursuit of 'development through integration' model. In this instance, the one cardinal pillar of this 'model' that needs to change is a shift from the pursuit of ideologically driven linear market integration models (à la Viner 1958) in favour of the establishment of an African continental integration agenda that sufficiently caters for the strategic interests of all participating Member States. This approach could significantly change the way integration has been approached thus far, and is likely to increase ownership and funding of the integration agenda by Africans themselves because it adopts an approach that goes beyond the desirability and benefits of a united continent and considers and offers actual benefits to membership and participation, thereby building a self-sustaining mechanism of progress into the continental integration edifice, which seems to be missing at the moment. African countries should therefore be encouraged identify and use their strategic self-interest and clearly identified benefits to be derived from integration as the main driving force that defines and determines the integration agenda .

The same 'strategic interests' logic or lack therefore could be applied to the AU Member States unwillingness to surrender the control of macroeconomic policy-making to a regional/continental authority, or to face potential consumption costs that may arise from importing from a high-cost member country, or to accept the unequal distribution of the gains and losses that may follow an integration agreement while discontinuing existing economic ties with non-members (Geda and Kebret 2007: 359). Some authors like Oyejide et al. (1999) have argued that African integration schemes suffer from endemic implementation lapses because of a lack of political will to carry out agreed commitments in the face of ensuring loss of national sovereignty, absence of adequate technical and management expertise, expectation of loss of fiscal revenue on trade taxes, and uncertainty over the distribution of the gains and losses of integration. Though this may indeed be a question of the lack of political will, it certainly comes across as the result of the benefits of integration not being perceived as higher than its associated costs (again the question of strategic interest not being clearly articulated and incorporated in the integration arrangement). Political expediency (for example, responding to urgent domestic needs with scarce resources under pressure from a constituency that has given a developmental mandate within a specific electoral cycle) may be the reason why there is a lack of political will to implement regional and continental-level commitments. Normally, countries have a clear domestic agenda that informs their international commitments and they pursue those commitments guided by their domestically defined prerogatives, discounting in the process their options and gains as they subscribe to every international agreement including the ones to which they are compelled by international agreements to comply. This is what sometimes makes the difference between high and low compliance but as can be expected, their own strategic interests as perceived and defined should normally drive their actions.

Apart from the challenge of the non-definition or incorporation of country's strategic interests in the design and implementation of Africa's regional integration arrangements, there also seems to be no consensus about the polity being created through the current integration efforts and even much less clarity about the most suitable pathway to be adopted or the most appropriate institutions to be created to accompany this process. A plan to establish a union government for Africa was launched at the 4th Ordinary Session of the Assembly of Heads of State and Government, held in Abuja, Nigeria, in January 2005. There the AU agreed to the proposals made by the Libyan government regarding the establishment of ministerial portfolios for the organisation. This proposal which had been made at the 6th Ordinary Session of the Executive Council of the AU recommended the establishment of the posts of an *African minister of Transport and Communications and a minister of Defence and Foreign Affairs*. This was intended to be a step towards *harmonising the transport and communications portfolios* of the continent under one ministry and also to have a common defence and foreign-affairs policy managed centrally. To follow up on this recommendation, the AU set up a committee which later convened a conference under the theme *the 'desirability of a Union Government of Africa'*. The conference came up with a number of key conclusions and recommendations. It acknowledged the need for an AU government made up of *a union of the people and not just a union of states and governments*. It however recommended that its creation must come about through the *principle of gradual incrementalism*; and that the role of the RECs as building blocks for the continental framework should be highlighted. Based on the findings of this conference, the Assembly mandated the AU Commission to prepare a consolidated framework document defining the purpose of the Union Government, its nature, scope, core values, steps and processes, as well as an indicative road map for its achievement.

In July 2006, a commission led by former president Obasanjo submitted a detailed report to the Commission entitled 'A Study on an African Union Government: Towards the United States of Africa' to the 7th Ordinary Session of the AU Assembly in Banjul, Gambia. The study identified 16 strategic areas that ought to be the focus of an AU government including: continental integration; education, training, skills development, science and technology; energy; environment; external relations; food, agriculture and water resources; gender and youth; governance and human rights; health; industry and mineral resources; finance; peace and security; social affairs and solidarity; sport and culture; a trade and customs union; and infrastructure, information technology and biotechnology (AU 2006: 8). The study also noted that the design and functioning of a Union Government as a tool for integration would have far-reaching implications on the existing institutions and programmes of the AU (AU 2006: 14). A statement which can lead to the plausible conclusion that the current programmes and institutions have not been conceived and are not being implemented expressly with the objective of building towards this desirable union government. For a process that started in 1963 to still be speaking of the desirability of the fruit of political integration in 2006 (more than four decades later on) speaks of an initiative that has been undertaken and driven without an agreed-upon destination nor broad consensus about how to proceed moving forward. This probably explains why the planned organs of the Union as foreseen in the Constitutive Act are taking forever to be established and those which have been established are underfunded and disempowered.

Since the submission of the report of the union government commission, not much seems to have been done in carrying their recommendations forward or in altering the functioning of the current institutions of integration to expressly start working towards the setting up of the union government. For Africa, political integration seems to be only an ideal that the AU Member States aspire towards but do not yet seem ready to take the necessary steps to move decisively in that direction. It further suggests that the ghosts of the Casablanca and Monrovia debates have not been completely laid to rest. Until recently headed by Libya's former leader Gaddafi, a group of some 20 states has been supporting the plan of a strong political union. These 'unionists' are opposed by the 'gradualists', who prefer an organic or gradual development. The 'gradualists' are in general opting for a process where economic integration in sub-regional groups should eventually lead to African unification.

Some would argue there is consensus about the importance of an integrated Africa but only disagreement about how to achieve this objective. To other analysts however, the disagreements about the pace and model of integration as well as the poor implementation record instead, point to a more fundamental problem associated with the conception and design of the existing set of African regional integration schemes and institutions. McCarthy (1999), for example, finds fault with both the conception and design of most of Africa's regional integration schemes. He argues that integration was conceptually designed as an inward-looking instrument of industrial development. In this context, the principal goal of integration and growth in intra-regional trade was for economic development and structural transformation through industrialisation; while the main role of integration was to aggregate the small individual economies into larger regional markets. Even though the formation of these larger integrated markets has remained elusive in most parts of the continent, this was a problematic approach to be adopted in the first place because though the 'new' regional economy would be larger than the individual economies, the combined markets would still not have been large enough to promote the high levels of industrial development promised by regional integration aspirations (Oyejide et al. 1999: 7)[1]. As such the economies of scale argument for the promotion of regional cooperation would have made for larger and hopefully more competitive markets but would not have led to large-scale industrialisation and economic transformation that these countries were hoping to benefit from regional cooperation without a structural transformation of their own national economies. To put things into perspective, Sub-Saharan Africa GDP for 2019 was $1,770.04B, a 2.8% increase from 2018. Sub-Saharan Africa GDP for 2018 was $1,721.89B, a 4.82% increase from 2017. Sub-Saharan Africa GDP for 2017 was $1,642.69B, a 6.51% increase from 2016. This means that If SSA were a single country/economy in 2021, it would have been only the tenth largest economy in the world, after much 'smaller' (in land size and population when compared to SSA) countries like Italy and Korea. They would not have been as large as the economies of Japan, Germany, France, the United Kingdom or Canada for that matter. However, these countries are single-entity polities under a single political authority and with the advantages of homogeneity in the coherence of policy action and efficiency of public institutions that can be derived from a single country to a level that no regional organisation or entity can dream of. See table 2.2:

This table and the associated figures challenge the larger market argument that underlies the question of African integration, the argument according to which, by combining their smaller economies, stand a better chance of being significant players on the global stage. Although there could be some merit to this argument, there is no doubt that concentrating to grow and develop the existing economies individually would lend greater strength and credence to

Table 2.2 Global Classification of Nominal GDP in Billions (USD)

	GDP (Nominal) (Billions of $)			
Country/Economy	*2020*	*Rank*	*2021*	*Rank*
United States	20,893.75	1	22,939.58	1
China	14,866.74	2	16,862.98	2
Japan	5,045.10	3	5,103.11	3
Germany	3,843.34	4	4,230.17	4
United Kingdom	2,709.68	5	3,108.42	5
India	2,660.24	6	2,946.06	6
France	2,624.42	7	2,940.43	7
Italy	1,884.94	8	2,120.23	8
Canada	1,644.04	9	2,015.98	9
Korea	1,638.26	10	1,823.85	10
Russia	1,478.57	11	1,647.57	11
Brazil	1,444.72	12	1,645.84	12
Australia	1,359.37	13	1,610.56	13
Spain	1,280.46	14	1,439.96	14
Mexico	1,073.92	15	1,285.52	15

Source: International Monetary Fund World Economic Outlook (October 2021).

this integration argument. The challenge comes when the growth and development is meant to also principally come from integration, whereas countries like Brazil or even Mexico as standalone entities are amongst the 15 largest economies in the world, even before becoming part of any regional integration arrangement. Africa would therefore have to recalibrate its discussion and debate on regional integration and the role it can meaningfully play in the growth and development efforts of its Member States and the region at large. This would probably have to start with a rethinking of its model of integration and the associated guiding philosophy and design.

In terms of the design up to this point, the preference seems to be for formal trade and factor market integration through the adoption of rather ambitious targets of regional integration, like the creation of customs unions and common market areas after the specific cutoff dates. These have not often taken into consideration the unfavourable structural factors characterising Africa, such as the competitive nature of primary production (including volatility of world market prices), small size, low per capita income, limited manufacturing capacity, weak financial sectors and poor (interstate and intrastate) transportation and communications infrastructure. These structural difficulties produce economies that have little to trade with each other but are locked into a North–South trading relationship, a reality which has given rise to regional arrangements that have the lowest levels of recorded intraregional trade of all integration experiences (McCarthy 1999: 21).

Hartzenberg (2011) also blames the poor implementation of Africa's regional economic integration arrangements on the paradigm of linear market integration marked by step-wise integration of goods, labour and capital markets, with eventual monetary and fiscal integration. Arguing that focussing on supply-side constraints through a deeper integration agenda that includes services, investment and competition policy (other than border issues like tariffs) may prove to be a more effective route for the promotion of integration. Motsamai and Qobo (2012) on the other hand identify three interlinked factors that limit regional integration processes in Africa and constrain its potential to be used as a vehicle for development in national economies, beneficial integration into the global economy and facilitating Pan-African Unity. These are centred on: *institutions of governance* including the structure of domestic politics, structural conditions of poorly developed economies and their dependence on one or two primary products, as well as the capacity to assert policy preferences in international economic relations.

These factors together explain why Africa's integration efforts have thus far yielded less than satisfactory results and in most cases are indicative of specific actions that could produce meaningful results for Africa's integration efforts. It is however unclear which of these challenges represents a significant enough pillar that could cause a huge turnaround in Africa's experience of integration. This strengthens the case for Africa's model of integration to be further interrogated and perhaps revisited with the objective of adopting alternative designs and paradigms. It is within this context that this proposal is introducing the developmental regionalism approach as a possible alternative paradigm to be adopted for Africa's integration. It however remains a debatable question whether the pursuit of developmental regionalism would be successful if fully adopted in Africa, because there has not really been a precedence of this approach to regional integration in any other parts of the world. The uniqueness of this approach lies in the attribution of developmental roles to regional and continental institutions of integration, which given the background and challenges common to some of these institutions, including resources and capacity constraints, may not be completely equipped to discharge the responsibilities that may come with being the main drivers of a development mandate aimed at the economic transformation of the continent. But again what options does the continent have to do with, since it has already adopted a model of integration that grants significant responsibility to regional institutions of integration to drive the integration process and bring about certain development outcomes while at it? The enormity and complexity of the challenge must however not serve as a discouraging factor, as looking at these identified challenges with innovative lenses surely holds the promise to bring positive change to Africa's integration and development experience.

SUMMARY AND CONCLUSION

Africa's experience of regional integration has in many ways fallen short of the expectations of its citizens and failed to meet their developmental aspirations. This chapter has presented a brief historical account of the origins of Africa's integration situated around the formation of the OAU, building upon a number of important Pan-Africanist conferences. The chapter has also presented some of the challenges common with Africa's practice of integration, beginning with the question of multiple membership to several regional integration arrangements and also mentioning possible challenges with the design and adoption of the linear market integration model. A significant argument has been the lack of consideration given to the strategic interest of participating Member States in regional integration arrangements, which reduces their ownership and willingness to fund regional arrangements, comparing them against domestic priorities and being unable to derive immediate economic or political benefits from participation in regional integration arrangements, apart from the somewhat romantic notion of the pursuit of African Unity. With this analysis, the chapter makes a case for the design and conceptualisation of Africa's model of integration to be revisited, opening up in the process the room for the consideration of a developmental regionalism paradigm. Though without a real global example of reference, it may still serve Africa better in fulfilling the expectations currently built into the successful attainment of the objectives of regional integration in Africa. To understand some of these objectives and expectations, the next chapter shall briefly present some of the key milestones and stated development objectives of some of Africa's main integration programs.

NOTE

1. Sub-Saharan Africa GDP for 2019 was $1,770.04B, a 2.8% increase from 2018. Sub-Saharan Africa GDP for 2018 was $1,721.89B, a 4.82% increase from 2017. Sub-Saharan Africa GDP for 2017 was $1,642.69B, a 6.51% increase from 2016.

Chapter 3

Key Milestones and Treaties Guiding Africa's Political and Economic Integration

INTRODUCTION

Ernst Haas the founder of the neofunctionalist approach, defines regional integration as the process whereby political actors in several distinct national settings are persuaded to shift their loyalties, expectations and political activities to a new centre, whose institutions possess or demand jurisdiction over pre-existing national states. The result is a new political community, superimposed over the pre-existing ones (Haas 1958: 16). Seen from this perspective, there is an expectation that the successful conduct of regional integration should entail transferring loyalty, expectations and decision-making power to a new, regional centre. By contrast, Karl Deutsch defined regional integration not as a process but rather a state of affairs: 'a relationship among units in which they are mutually interdependent and jointly produce system properties which they would separately lack' (Deutsch 1968: 192). These divergent conceptualisations of regional integration add to the notion that the unfolding of any regional integration project like the one currently unfolding in Africa could adopt different routes to get certain desirable outcomes. For Africa, their trajectory has been informed by its political history of colonisation and continued economic challenges for the last couple of decades.

This chapter makes the argument that Africa's approach and practice of integration was greatly influenced by the early formalisations of regionalism introduced in the 1950s–1960s by political economists like Viner (1950) and Balassa (1961). These scholars viewed integration as a gradual process of economic cooperation following an inherent linearity in five concrete steps, beginning with the formation of a Free Trade Area (FTA), proceeding to a customs union, a common market, an economic union and a political union (Balassa 1961). This conceptualisation of regional integration has been and remains at the heart of Africa's practice of market integration. In this regard, the principal milestones have been the creation of the Organisation of African Unity (OAU) (1963), the adoption of the Lagos Plan of Action (LPA), the adoption of the Abuja Treaty, the conversion of the OAU to the African Union (AU) and to a certain extent the creation of the New Partnership for Africa's Development (NEPAD) development agency, all the way up to the adoption of the African Continental Free Trade Area (AFCFTA). Far from being an exhaustive list of the important programs of key moments of Africa's integration journey, these selected components capture more or less the legal and institutional framework upon which the economic integration and development mandate of Africa's integration sits. For completeness, and to be able to place a context to the main thesis of this volume, it is important to briefly present some important components of these different milestones with the objective of highlighting the specific contributions they make and have made in defining Africa's integration trajectory thus far. This shall hopefully present some background and context to understanding some of the earlier mentioned challenges, while at the same time giving context to the developmental regionalism adoption proposal. These shall be presented under the subheading of the key economic milestones in Africa's integration, in the section that follows.

KEY ECONOMIC INTEGRATION MILESTONES IN AFRICA

From a historical perspective, there have been arguably five critical milestones moments that have shaped the continent's economic integration trajectory. These include the formation of the OAU in 1963, the adoption of the LPA and the Final Act of Lagos (FAL) in 1980, the adoption of the Abuja Treaty establishing the African Economic Community (AEC) in 1991 and the establishment of the AU in 2001, including the creation of the NEPAD and the adoption of the AFCFTA in 2018. The OAU charter and the Constitutive Act establishing the AU define regional integration as one of the anchoring ideals of African unity. The LPA and the Abuja Treaty establishing the AEC spell out the economic, political and institutional mechanisms for attaining this ideal, while NEPAD has been defined as the overarching development framework for the region (UNECA 2004: 1). Together these constitute the policy framework within which the continent's integration is being pursued. They provide the context for fostering the political and economic integration of Africa driven by the AU and its institutions. An examination of the contribution of these different initiatives to the advancement of continental integration is important for the overall objectives of this volume, which is why these are briefly examined in the subsections that follow.

The Organisation of African Unity

The Organization of African Unity (OAU) was created to promote unity and solidarity amongst African states. It was intended to serve as a platform to coordinate the efforts to achieve a better life for the peoples of Africa (OAU 1981). This greater cooperation amongst African states was to be achieved through the coordination and harmonisation of their policies in a number of areas, particularly through the promotion of political, diplomatic and economic cooperation. According to Article 2 of the OAU charter, the purpose of the organisation was, amongst others: to promote the unity and solidarity of the African states; to defend their sovereignty, their territorial integrity and independence; to eradicate all forms of colonialism from Africa and to promote international cooperation having due regard to the charter of the United Nations and the Universal Declaration of Human Rights. The main avenue for the accomplishment of these objectives was policy coordination and cooperation in a number of spheres including: political and diplomatic cooperation; economic cooperation, including transport and communications; educational and cultural cooperation; health, sanitation and nutritional cooperation; scientific and technical cooperation and cooperation for defence and security.

The aspirations towards greater cooperation were partly side-lined by the organisation's preoccupation with the fight for the total liberation of the continent from colonialism and apartheid in South Africa. This remained a core objective that drove the OAU, from its inception in 1963 to 1975. During this period, the OAU was mainly concerned with (a) the inter-state conflicts that took place at the time, and (b) with political support to the struggle for eradicating racist and colonial rule in southern Africa.(Bujra 2002). This gave the continental organisation a largely political focus in the first decade of its operation with less attention given to issues of economic integration.

The economic performance of African countries in the 1970s, and the persistence of conflict, poverty and under-development after the first decade of the OAU's existence accentuated by the 1973 global economic crisis convinced African leaders of the need to shift the focus of their continental coordination efforts towards the economic emancipation of the continent (Bujra 2002). This led to a number of meetings, seminars and brainstorming sessions organised both by the OAU and the United Nation's Economic Commission for Africa (UNECA). At the eleventh extraordinary session of the OAU council of ministers in 1976, the Kinshasa Declaration was made which recommended the free ownership and control of natural resources by ensuring permanent sovereignty of African countries, the establishment of multinational companies, the establishment of the African Common Market, the African Energy Commission, and the AEC within a period of 15 to

20 years (Kouassi 2007: 3). Through this declaration it can be argued that the concept of economic autonomy and collective self-reliance by African countries was promoted by the OAU as a development paradigm to be embraced for the continental integration project. Integration (it was intended) would contribute in redressing the continent's underdevelopment and grant it a more significant place on the world stage. Attaining integration in these chosen areas would also facilitate coordinated development and in so doing uplift the continent as a whole.

This belief in the importance of collective self-reliance gave rise to the Monrovia Declaration in 1979, a commitment by heads of state and government to measure and lead reforms aimed at achieving national and collective self-reliance in economic and social development for the establishment of a new international economic order (OAU 1979). The declaration promoted the social and economic development and integration of African economies with a view to achieving an increasing measure of self-reliance and self-sustainment. Leaders also committed themselves to establishing national, sub-regional and regional institutions that would facilitate the attainment of the objectives of self-reliance and self-sustainment.

These statements of intent should be understood within the context of the continent's history of colonisation that had left most countries with a weak economic base, dependent upon a few raw materials and struggling to be competitive on the global stage. With this declaration, African leaders gave the continental integration project an economic focus based on the principles of solidarity and mutual dependence. This was to be actualised through economic cooperation in a range of areas with an emphasis on the use of Africa's resources for the benefit of its citizens. States also went ahead to articulate their vision of regional and sub-regional cooperation that would constitute the building blocks for continental integration. They consequently gave a task to the OAU secretariat to convene a meeting to develop a policy document on economic development and cooperation on the continent, which is what the LPA became when it was drafted and adopted.

The Lagos Plan of Action

The LPA based its strategies on key principles aimed at building an alternative form of development for Africa. Accordingly, self-reliance was the corner pillar and basis of development – at the national, sub-regional and regional levels, and equity in the distribution of wealth at the national level became a fundamental objective of development. On the basis of these principles, the LPA gave primacy to the development of agriculture (first for food and then for export), industrialisation (to satisfy basic needs), mining industries (to recover total and permanent sovereignty over national resources and establish mineral-based industries), human resources and science and technology (Bujra 2002). Accordingly, the LPA encouraged the pursuit of three goals: (i) high and sustained economic growth; (ii) transformation of the economic and social structures; and, (iii) maintenance of a sustainable resource base. Adedeji (2002) has argued that the LPA promoted a model of regionalism that involved six mutually interdependent processes:

i) the integration of the physical, institutional and social infrastructure;
ii) the integration of the production structures
iii) market integration
iv) resolution of inter-country conflicts and prevention of acts of political destabilisation;
v) ensuring stability and security, both at nation-state and inter-country levels; and
vi) the creation of an enabling environment for initiative and enterprise as well as facilitating cross-border factor movements.

The FAL set out an implementation schedule for this plan of action in two stages of 10 years each. African states thus committed themselves in the first 10-year (1980–1990) period to:

- strengthening the existing regional economic communities (RECs) and establishing other economic groupings in the other regions of Africa, to cover the continent as a whole (Central Africa, Eastern Africa, Southern Africa, Northern Africa);
- enhancing sectoral integration at the continental level, and particularly in the fields of agriculture, food, transport, and communications, industry and energy;
- Promoting coordination and harmonisation among the existing and future economic groupings for a gradual establishment of an African Common Market.

During the second 10-year period (1990–2000) they further committed to:

- taking steps for further sectoral integration through: harmonisation of their strategies, policies and economic development plans; promotion of joint projects, particularly in the above-mentioned economic fields and the harmonisation of their financial and monetary policies;
- adopting measures to establish an African Common Market and other measures that would lead to the attainment of the aims and objectives of the AEC.

The FAL also detailed out a plan of action to accomplish these objectives and acknowledged that the starting point should be the strengthening of existing sub-regional economic groupings and the establishment of new ones where deemed desirable. To this end, they authorised the drafting of the treaty for the establishment of the AEC whose aim would be to promote collective and accelerated self-reliant and self-sustaining development cooperation among the states and their integration in the economic, social and cultural fields. That treaty was subsequently signed in Abuja in June 1991 and is commonly known just as the Abuja Treaty (Adedeji 2002).

The Abuja Treaty

The Abuja Treaty, also known as the treaty for the establishment of an AEC, was ratified in 1991 with the following objectives:

i) To promote economic, social and cultural development and the integration of African economies in order to increase economic self-reliance and promote an endogenous and self-sustained development.
ii) To establish, on a continental scale, a framework for the development, mobilisation and utilisation of the human and material resources of Africa in order to achieve a self-reliant development.
iii) To promote cooperation in all fields of human endeavour in order to raise the standard of living of African peoples, and maintain and enhance economic stability, foster close and peaceful relations among Member States and contribute to the progress, development and economic integration of the continent.
iv) To coordinate and harmonise policies among existing and future economic communities in order to foster the gradual establishment of the AEC.

The treaty made provision for gradual integration of Africa through the progressive incorporation of its existing RECs. It recognised the coordination, harmonisation and integration of Africa's RECs as a prerequisite to their serving as building blocks for the creation of an African Common Market by 2028. Under this treaty, the creation of a full-fledged AEC was set to be accomplished over a period of 34 years (1994–2028) in six stages, ending in an economic union with a common currency, full mobility of factors of production and free trade among the continent's 53 countries (UNECA 2006). The objectives that were to be accomplished at every stage as well as the progress registered until recently are briefly presented in table 3.1:

Table 3.1 indicates that there has been progress in attaining the first stage objective of strengthening the institutional frameworks of existing RECs

Table 3.1 Africa's Integration Progress Relative to Abuja Treaty Objectives

Objectives	*Target Date*	*Progress Till Date*
1st Stage: (5 years) Strengthen RECs	1999	Achieved
2nd Stage (8 years) Coordinate and harmonise activities and progressively eliminate tariff and nontariff barriers	2007	Partially achieved
3rd Stage (10 years) Free Trade Area and Customs Union in each REC.	2017	Partially achieved
3rd Stage (10 years) Free Trade Area and Customs Union in each REC.	2017	Partially achieved
4th Stage (2 years) Continental Custom Union.	2019	Not achieved
5th Stage (4 years). Continental Common Market.	2023	Not achieved but African Continental Free Trade Area CFTA Launched January 2018, Common Market unlike by 2023
6th Stage (5 years) Continental Economic and Monetary Union	2028	Target date still ahead.

Source: Author's Compilation.

and creating others where they did not exist. There has also been progress in the second stage related to the coordination and harmonisation of certain activities and elimination of tariffs and nontariff barriers, though not in all RECs. Some RECs are more advanced in the attainment of FTAs, namely the Common Market for East and Southern Africa (COMESA), the East African Community (EAC), the Economic Community of Central African States (ECCAS), the Economic Community of West African States (ECOWAS) and the Southern African Development Community (SADC). COMESA and EAC have gone a step further and initiated the establishment of a Customs Union, whereas in the south the Southern African Customs Union (SACU) has been operational for a long time (UNECA 2012: 5). COMESA has managed to simplify its custom procedures and eliminated some nontariff barriers (in particular import licensing), the removal of foreign exchange restrictions and the removal of import and export quotas (UNCTAD 2009: 14). Through these milestone objectives and pursuant of the objectives outlined in the LPA, the Abuja Treaty laid out the continental vision for economic and political integration. It marked a significant milestone in expressing a desired destination for African cooperation and, though progress and implementation challenges have been registered, it has nevertheless produced a map and set targets against which the progress of continental integration could be gauged. It also established the framework within which further cooperation and continental integration would be expected to deliver on Africa's economic development aspirations. These targets remain today the yardstick often used to justify the lack of progress in Africa's integration and, by proxy, the failure of integration initiatives to deliver on developmental promises.

The performance of Africa's institutions of integration has traditionally come under scrutiny, mostly in relation to their contribution to the accomplishment of these objectives. The OAU, for example, was greatly criticised for being little more than a collaboration of governments of sovereign states that placed an unfair amount of emphasis on preserving and protecting their national sovereignty. An organisation that did not interfere in the internal affairs of its members, refrained from criticising the actions of other governments in public and showed no seriousness in the pooling of sovereignty (Landsberg 2012: 6). These weaknesses in advancing a deepening integration agenda on the continent was coupled with the fact that the resolutions and programmes of the 1980s, as well as those passed in the 1990s, did not produce significant results in improving the economic situation of Africa (Bujra 2002). In the decade following the adoption of the Abuja Treaty, given the persistent economic challenges witnessed by most countries on the continent, the integration agenda developed a new imperative for adopting a different political and economic orientation to the continent's cooperation and this ushered in the birth of the AU and the NEPAD.

The African Union and NEPAD

The OAU was replaced by the AU through a Constitutive Act of 2000, which also established a new blueprint for Africa's socioeconomic development – the NEPAD, formally adopted in 2001. NEPAD represented a shift in paradigm from previous initiatives on the continent because it recognised the link between development on the one hand, and governance, democratisation and peace and security as important pillars for the success of Africa's integration project on the other. It also placed the challenge of poverty alleviation and addressing underdevelopment at the core of a 'new' Pan-Africanism in Africa (Landsberg 2008: 208).

Both the AU and NEPAD represented a fresh impetus towards the attainment of the objective of an AEC by 2028 (Mukamunana and Moeti 2005: 95). Like its predecessor the OAU, the AU was founded with the objective of achieving greater unity and solidarity between the African countries and the peoples of Africa, defending the sovereignty, territorial integrity and independence of its Member States and accelerating the political and socioeconomic integration of the continent. It also adopted the objective of promoting and defending African common positions on issues of interest to the continent and its peoples, encouraging international cooperation, and promoting peace, security and stability on the continent.

The AU was meant to bring about a different political orientation to the integration process in that it moved away from some of the principles that had governed and guided its predecessor, the OAU, like that of non-interference in the internal affairs of Member States. This different political orientation is captured in Article 4 of the Constitutive Act, which advocates for a common defence policy, popular participation in the affairs of the Union and the right to intervene directly in a member state country in the case of crimes against humanity and the right to intervene to restore peace and security in a Member State at its request (Kouassi 2007: 18). The optimism that accompanied the birth of the AU prompted some observers (see Landsberg 2012) to talk about new 'continentalism', a policy revolution accompanied by the continent's subscription to a new set of norms, principles, values, mechanisms and structures, different from those characterised under the OAU. This new wave of inter-African cooperation put the issues of development, governance, democratisation, economic growth, and peace and security firmly on the continental agenda (Landsberg 2012: 2).

The AU principles also departed from its predecessor by bringing a new focus on *good governance* and the *protection of human rights*. With these the AU set for itself the objective of promoting democratic principles and institutions, popular participation and good governance and promoting and protecting human and peoples' rights in accordance with the African Charter on Human and Peoples' Rights and other relevant human rights instruments (OAU 2000). Though embracing these new principles, the AU did not completely abandon some of the ones identified in the OAU as it sought to enhance institutional and policy continuity between the two institutions. Such search for continuity had earlier been captured in the Sirte Declaration of 1999, wherein African leaders committed themselves to establishing a union that will be in conformity with the objectives of the OAU Charter and to accelerate the process of the implementation of the Treaty Establishing the AEC by inter alia shortening the implementation periods set out in the Abuja Treaty and ensuring the speedy establishment of all the institutions provided for in the treaty like the African Central Bank, the African Monetary Union, the African Court of Justice and the Pan-African Parliament (Biswaro 2011: 396).

The search for continuity meant that a number of legal instruments adopted under the OAU were carried over to the AU like the Cairo Declaration on the mechanism for the prevention, management and resolution of conflict, the African Charter on Human and People's Rights and the protocol on the relations between the OAU and the RECs (Kouassi 2007: 18). In some regards, the founding of the AU represented continuity with the momentum that had been developed through the OAU, albeit with the modifications of certain principles and concepts that were both relevant and in sync with the developmental challenges of the continent in the twenty-first century, in particular its focus on development and growth.

NEPAD had the main objective to meet the challenge of eradicating poverty from Africa, through the establishment of a stable environment conducive to peace and security and the promotion of sustainable economic growth and development, in order to ensure the continent's full participation in global political and economic affairs (Kouassi 2007: 21). It has also been described as the continent's 'market driven, extra-regional partnership model' depicting the extent to which it contrasts with the inward-looking/self-sufficient developmental paradigms adopted in the 1970s and enshrined in the philosophy of the OAU (Ikome 2007: 20). It is governed by a three-tier structure; an implementation committee (assembly of Heads of State responsible for implementation), a steering committee (representatives of members of the implementation committee) and the NEPAD Secretariat responsible for the coordination of NEPAD programmes. The responsibility for its implementation however remains with Member States and in partnership with the private sector, civil society and the RECs, following the principle of subsidiarity. The secretariat facilitates the implementation of programmes by (amongst others) mobilising resources and political support, carrying out advocacy and promotion campaigns and promoting institutional coordination in programme implementation (Kouassi 2007: 23). Some of its current flagship programmes include the initiative on peace, security, democracy and political governance (under which the African Peer Review Mechanism falls), closing the infrastructure gap (promoting investment in infrastructure in energy, transport, water and sanitation including information and communications technology) and an initiative on human resources development including a reversal of the trend towards the brain drain. NEPAD therefore represents a new approach to the pursuit of Africa's economic integration and development based on greater cooperation with the rest of the world and the inputting of more responsibilities to African leaders on issues of governance and accountability to their citizens.

The establishment of the AU undoubtedly generated new dynamism towards regional cooperation. It was founded amidst the realisation that the efforts of close to four decades of continental integration had not yielded much in terms of developmental benefits to the continent. At the time of the demise of the OAU and the birth of the AU, Africa was virtually imploding because of internal and external pressures, including conflicts, poverty, under-development and public health crisis like malaria, tuberculosis and HIV/AIDS (Biswaro

2011: 396). As has been argued by the 2009 Economic Development in Africa Report:

> regional integration, when designed and implemented within a broader development strategy to promote economic diversification, structural changes and technological development, could enhance productive capacities of African economies, realise economies of scale, improve competiveness and serve as a launching pad for African economies' effective participation in the global economy. (UNCTAD 2009)

It can also be observed that the pursuit of political and economic integration in the AU's approach to integration has not been dissociated from each other. This somewhat reflects the neofunctionalist belief that greater economic integration when accompanied by the creation of functional supranational-styled institutions is likely to lead to eventual political integration. This probably explains why Africa's pursuit of economic integration has been mostly driven as a political process and accompanied by the creation of a number of institutions intended to push forward the integration agenda. However, these created institutions without adequate financial resources and the transfer of certain sovereign competencies from AU Member States to the continental bodies; it will be very difficult for them to drive and push forward the integration agenda.

The African Continental Free Trade Area

According to the 2021 UNCTAD Economic Development in Africa Report, the AFCFTA is expected to be a game changer for development ambitions in Africa. This is because it arrives at a crucial time when African countries are dealing with increased poverty levels and socioeconomic setbacks due to the coronavirus disease pandemic and its related financial, climatic and food-related shocks. As the report argues, the design of the agreement establishing the AFCFTA reflects an explicit commitment to create a framework for deeper socioeconomic integration and improved cooperation that enables trade, investment and the mobility of people, to support industrialisation and the development of a dynamic services sector. As per the founding charters, the general objectives of the AFCFTA are the following:

i) To create a single market for goods and services, facilitated by the movement of persons in order to deepen the economic integration of the African continent and in accordance with the Pan-African Vision of 'An integrated, prosperous and peaceful Africa' enshrined in Agenda 2063.

ii) To create a liberalised market for goods and services through successive rounds of negotiations.
iii) To contribute to the movement of capital and natural persons and facilitate investments building on the initiatives and developments in the State Parties and RECs.
iv) To lay the foundation for the establishment of a Continental Customs Union at a later stage.
v) To promote and attain sustainable and inclusive socioeconomic development, gender equality and structural transformation of the State Parties.
vi) To enhance the competitiveness of the economies of State Parties within the continent and the global market.
vii) To promote industrial development through diversification and regional value chain development, agricultural development and food security.

This AFCFTA was launched on 21 March 2018 at a Summit of the AU, held in Kigali, Rwanda. According to UNECA (2017), the CFTA will bring together 54 African countries with a combined population of more than one billion people and a combined gross domestic product of more than US $3.4 trillion. It has the potential to boost intra-African trade by 52% by 2022. The objective of the CFTA is to create a single market for goods and services, facilitated by the movement of persons in order to deepen the economic integration of the African continent and in accordance with the Pan African Vision of 'An integrated, prosperous and peaceful Africa' enshrined in Agenda 2063. The CFTA has been welcomed with much enthusiasm in a similar manner as comparable initiatives have been received on the continent with optimism around the contribution that they are expected to make to the continent's economic integration and development efforts. Mevel and Karingi (2013) have modelled the impact of the CFTA with the removal of all tariffs on trade between African countries and supplemented their analysis with the implied effects of improved trade facilitation between African countries using a database on trade costs. They find that the trade creation effects of the CFTA would exceed and more than compensate for trade diversion effects. According to their analysis, under the CFTA reform, intra-African trade is estimated to increase by 52.3% ($34.6 billion), compared with a baseline scenario without a CFTA, in 2022. In addition to this, Africa's industrial exports are forecasted to enjoy the highest gains, expanding by 53.3% ($27.9 billion). Their study also finds flanking the CFTA with trade facilitation measures would be important in maximising the impact of the CFTA on Africa's industrialisation and ensuring that all countries gain from the CFTA. The UNCTAD (2021) Economic Development in Africa report has argued in this regard that the AFCFTA could reduce COVID-19-induced growth contraction, poverty and inequality trends and spur sustainable and inclusive growth on the continent if stronger support measures targeting women, young traders and small businesses are implemented. The same report shows that trade policies alone are unlikely to support inclusive economic growth on the continent. Other measures are needed to increase the potential distributional gains from regional integration and help ensure inclusive development. Some of the possible measures could include cooperation in promoting investment and competition policies, accelerating financing of infrastructure that facilitates rural–urban linkages and providing equal access to socioeconomic opportunities and productive resources.

Similarly, the 2017 Economic Commission for Africa (ECA) report on 'Assessing Regional Integration in Africa VIII' had earlier described the Continental Free Trade Area (CFTA) as the flagship project of the AU's Agenda 2063 and a key initiative that would boost the industrialisation and economic development of the continent. The report argued that the CFTA had the potential to boost intra-African trade, stimulate investment and innovation, foster structural transformation, improve food security, enhance economic growth and export diversification and rationalise the overlapping trade regimes of the main RECs (UNECA 2017: xi). There is therefore no doubt that there is much enthusiasm and expectations attached to this new initiative and it will be interesting to see how much of these expectations are converted to real results as forecasted in the next couple of years. For this to happen, it is critically important that the AU does a few things differently from how it has conducted business in the past, including changing a few paradigms and approaches it has adopted thus far in its approach to the pursuit of economic integration, including changing its paradigm of integration and adopting a developmental regionalism approach, as shall be argued in chapter 5.

CONCLUSION

Africa has certainly come a long way from the days of the creation of the OAU to some of its current contemporary initiatives that promote regional integration. There is evidence of a lot of lesson drawing and adaption to the changing global economic and trade realities as the continent consistently strives to improve and assert itself on the global stage. From the earlier periods of the often termed 'dark ages' where the continent was riddled with poverty, disease, starvation and conflict, the turn of the new century has given rise to a new hope and commitment to do a few things differently. Earlier economic integration initiatives like the LPA and the Abuja Treaty have served as the foundation and building blocks of the continent's economic prosperity and integration but these are being augmented by new initiatives like the development focus that came with the creation of NEPAD and the optimism that now surrounds the adoption of the CFTA. From all these endeavours there seems to be evidence of the willingness to change, adapt, innovate and do a few things differently. Worth highlighting at the number of innovative perspectives being proposed alongside the CFTA. As the 2021 UNCTAD Economic Development in Africa Report has argued, the CFTA would be value-adding if it placed a greater emphasis on deeper intraregional trade, cross-border investments in infrastructure and fostered a 'made in Africa' trade and industrialisation policies. The report further argues that this is key to the continent's future prosperity and resilience to global financial, food-related, climatic and pandemic-related shocks. There is hope that the AFCFTA is going to be a game changer, if countries in Africa adopt policies that enhance consistency between trade measures, diversification objectives and inclusivity. Unless this is accomplished, the FTA may be restricted to a trade liberalisation agenda and may not fulfil the hopes and aspirations of the people of Africa. Such perspectives are at the heart of and aligned with the developmental regionalism approach and agenda being proposed in this volume, and another contribution that this volume intends to make in advancing the debate on Africa's development and economic integration objectives. If indeed it is effectively implemented, the AFCFTA can also help address challenges emanating from the excessive reliance in Africa on the supply of primary commodities and goods embodying limited value added to world markets – thus resolving also in the process the industrialisation question for Africa, which in itself is imperative for the economic transformation of the continent, releasing in the process the mutually reinforcing forces of greater market integration and industrialisation to sustain and benefit from the same. This will be an ultimate 'A game' in terms of outcomes for the economic integration agenda on the African continent. This is possible as shall be argued and elaborated in the next couple of chapters, beginning with a brief comparison of Africa's integration experience with that of the European Union's.

Chapter 4

A Comparison of Europe's and Africa's Experiences of Regional Integration

INTRODUCTION

One would immediately wonder why a comparison between Africa's and Europe's experiences of integration in the middle of a volume that focuses on proposing a change of paradigm for Africa's approach to its economic integration project. The justification for adopting this approach is twofold, the first being that the European Union (EU) of integration is often upheld as the normative or authoritative model of integration judged from the functioning of its created institutions and mostly influenced by the fact that it is by far the most extensively researched and documented experience of integration thanks to the advancement and progress of European Studies as a discipline. The second and more compelling reason, related to the experience of Africa is the fact that some scholars often argue that much of Africa's approach to integration is a combination of lesson drawing, copying, normative emulation and/or outright mimicry of the EU model of integration. The justification of this argument is often drawn from the similarities in the names of some of their institutions of integration although there are often sharp contrasts when it comes to the functioning of these institutions. If Europe can be considered (rightfully or debatably) as a good reference for regional integration, how does Africa's experience of integration compare or contrast with that of Europe, what are the major differences in the setup and functioning of their institutions of integration and what are the implications of these differences for the African Union's (AU's) own integration paradigm and models.

The paradox of dissimilar integration and cooperation trajectories that has resulted in the creation of similar institutions of integration with remarkable differences in their functioning and contribution to the integration outcomes remains a puzzle that has attracted many explanations. By placing the institutions and policy frameworks of the EU and the AU side by side it is possible to establish that the many similarities between the EU and the AU institutions of integration are mainly a case of 'institutional isomorphism' rather than a genuine adaptation of the key fundamentals of European integration, since both experiences have a different historical origin and have been influenced by different ideological paradigms.

In the case of Europe, neofunctionalism probably exercised the greatest influence. It was premised on a number of key principles, including the recognition of the importance of politics in regional integration, a liberal-pluralist conception of power, bargaining by regionally oriented pressure groups, the notion of task expansion and spillover (tendency of regional groups to expand the scope of issues areas and to move from cooperation in 'low politics' to cooperation in high politics) and the notion of the political community as an end production of regional integration (Acharya and Johnston 2007: 4). The 'organic' or stepwise creation of a 'supranational' entity is also the preoccupation of neofunctionalism. In its essence, neofunctionalism emphasises the mechanisms of technocratic decision-making, incremental change and learning processes. It also attaches considerable importance to the autonomous influence of supranational institutions and the emerging role of organised interests. Neofunctionalists on their part made the argument that the work of important political groups whose interest favour integration drive functional cooperation amongst Member States. If they perceived their interests were advanced in one area of cooperation, they would be inclined to attempt more of the same in other related areas, the so-called 'neofunctional spill over' (Ginsberg 2010: 66). A combination of these factors gives rise to a political space wherein institutions are created on the back of national political mechanisms but endowed with the built-in incentives and mechanisms to drive the integration agenda, which was not the case for Africa's own integration trajectory. This may perhaps explain why their own institutions of integration function differently from those of the EU, and it is important to understand these differences before proceeding to make recommendations about what needs to change in Africa's own approach and paradigm of integration.

A COMPARISON OF EUROPEAN UNION AND AFRICAN UNION INTEGRATION EXPERIENCES

Although the EU and the AU have had two different trajectories towards regional cooperation and integration, their divergent experiences have however led to the adoption of what may seem like identical institutional frameworks though with significant functional differences (similarly named institutions but different endowments and different functions). Bach (2008: 357), for example, argues that the institutional architecture of the AU departs from that of the EU in so far as decision-making within the AU is still strictly based on intergovernmentalism, devoid of sovereignty transfers and clear-cut enforcement mechanisms. In this regard, the AU is different from the EU in that its institutions are not yet endowed with supranational powers that would give them the neofunctionalist mandate and authority to drive integration in Africa as some of Europe's institutions do, through, for example, making and enforcing laws at the continental level as happens in Europe and bringing noncomplaint Member States to account at the European Court of Justice. There are in fact a few templates through which the experiences of the EU and AU integration can be compared. This may include their process/trajectory of integration (which is seen as linear by traditional theories and fuzzy by new approaches), their institutional structures (formal and informal), their style and approaches to leadership and leadership responsibilities (state-centric and diffused), their criteria and assertion to community membership (inclusive and exclusive), their economic and social drivers of integration (trade, market integration, and cultural/social cohesion), and the extent of their pooling of sovereignty as opposed to the degrees of cooperation. In this regard, there are clear observable similarities and differences between the EU and the AU's integration trajectories as presented in table 4.1:

It is clear from the table that the integration experiences of Europe and Africa have evolved differently. Going beyond symbolic resemblances in a few aspects, Europe and Africa embody two complex examples of regional governance, largely shaped by distinct logics. They may share a few generic similarities but are different in more ways. Both regions may have adopted the word 'union' and are led by a Commission and Councils, and each has a Parliament, but when one looks at the actual drivers, approaches, principles and modalities of regionalisation, it becomes clear that neither Europe nor Africa followed clearly defined linear paths to integration and that differences are certainly more significant than similarities. In both Europe and Africa, the threat to the well-being of their citizens was a factor that triggered the desire for more cooperation. Though admittedly, Europe and Africa adopted different routes to address the perceived threats to their security and well-being.

Though their methods and approach to greater cooperation and move towards integration may have been different, they both share the aspiration of improving upon the welfare of their citizens (through various forms of economic integration) and exercising a greater influence on the global scene by collective self-reliance (Axline 1994). The similarities in their objective and aspirations seem obvious if one were to examine the key policy documents creating their respective economic communities (Rome Treaty 1957

Table 4.1 Comparison of Europe and Africa's Integration Experiences

Comparative Indicator	*European Union*	*African Union*
Nature of institutions and regional organisations	Supranational and intergovernmental	Intergovernmental coordination and cooperation and a Secretariat with technocrats and senior officials elected from RECs
Process of regionalism	Incremental from ECSC to EU	Progressive political cooperation and slow economic/market integration
Conditions of membership	Conditional: Governance, human rights and democracy and some macroeconomic and social standards.	All-inclusive, security and conflicts resolution, market integration and some governance elements being introduced like the African Peer Review Mechanism (APRM).
Approach to sovereignty	Follows the principle of subsidiarity, with strong supranational EU institutions sharing some competencies with Member States in some areas, while Member States retain exclusive competencies in other areas	Member States are driven through intergovernmental cooperation, and deputised representation in Secretariat through Council of Representatives and Council of Ministers.
Drivers (economic, political and social fields)	Trade driven with single market and common currency, social policy and political dimension.	Political considerations with OAU, trade and market concerns with AEC but no social policy component
Type of regional leadership	Strong Foreign Secretary and Presidents of EU Parliament and Commission. With some leading Member States like Germany and France.	Rotational Presidency with leading agendas and an enlarged Secretariat with coordination and program management responsibilities.
Regional identity	Progressive construction of a European identity	Pan-Africanism and African solidarity as predominant ideologies.

Source: Author's compilation.

and Abuja Treaty of 1991). According to these treaties, both continents share a number of similar aspirations and approaches to their integration project. For starters, the agreements reached in each case are between the 'High Contracting parties' to form an (African/European) Economic Community. Both projects share the aspiration of improving the standards of living of their citizens (Article 2 RT and Article 4 AT) and to foster close (and peaceful in the case of the AT) relations among their Member States. They expressed their aspiration to form a common market thereby embracing trade liberalisations with the elimination of custom duties and all nontariff barriers (including quantitative restrictions) amongst members. Both treaties also advocated for the establishment of a common market with a transitional period and to be put into effect in stages. They also each advocated for some form of social policy, with the Rome Treaty adopting the European Social Fund for employment and an improvement in standards of living while the Abuja Treaty advocated for the adoption of Community Solidarity Development and Compensation (CSDC) funds which were in a sense similar to the European Regional Development Funds.

From this cursory examination of the two frameworks for the development of economic communities in Europe and Africa, the similarities in aspirations, ideology and approach are evident. This sort of mirroring has occurred notwithstanding the noted differences in the historical trajectory and eventual practise of cooperation by the two. The fact that the Abuja Treaty of 1991 came more than 30 years after the Rome Treaty (1957) would have given the Abuja Treaty a few years to see the fruits and results of the implementation of the Rome Treaty and draw a leaf or two in lessons learnt while designing its own treaty for the creation of an African Economic Community. However, both experiences have set up institutions that play different roles in driving their integration agenda. The difference in the setup, resource endowments and operations of these similar-looking institutions may hold the key to their effectiveness in driving the integration agenda. Furthermore, looking at the setup and functioning of these institutions, having noted the many significant ways in which both experiences differ plays into the neofunctionalist argument and expectations that institutions are important in successfully driving the deepening integration agenda. If institutions drive integration as per neofunctionalist argument, then it is important to understand how they have been set up and how they function, so as to build a realistic expectation about the role that can reasonably be attributed to them in pushing forward the integration agenda, especially from an African perspective. Therefore before making recommendations about a change in paradigm and approach towards the adoption of developmental regionalism, it is important to understand the institutional context within which these recommendations shall be operating. This shall be done by first examining the AU institutions of integration in the section that follows and following that with an examination of the functioning of the EU's own institutions of integration.

AN OVERVIEW OF AFRICA'S INSTITUTIONS OF INTEGRATION

The pursuit of Africa's unity and the integration of the continent has been accompanied by the creation of a number of institutions that are called upon to play a major role in the promotion of the further integration of the continent. These are the institutions identified by Article 7 of the Abuja Treaty (1993) as the organs of the African Economic Community, which include: (a) The Assembly of Heads of State and Government; (b) The Council of Ministers; (c) The Pan-African Parliament; (d) The Economic and Social Commission; (e) The Court of Justice; (f) The General Secretariat; and (g) The Specialised Technical Committees (STCs). When the Organisation of African Unity (OAU) became the AU in 2001, these organs became known as the organs of the union with a few more additions. According to Article 4 of the Constitutive Act of the AU, the organs of the union shall be the following: (a) The Assembly of the Union; (b) The Executive Council; (c) The Pan-African Parliament; (d) The Court of Justice; (e) The Commission; (f) The Permanent Representatives' Committee (PRC); (g) The STCs; (h) The Economic, Social and Cultural Council; (i) The Financial Institutions.

While these institutions are foreseen as part of the continental integration project, not all of them have been completely set up or are fully operational. However, the role that they are expected to play in the continent's integration project has been clearly articulated in a number of policy documents as summarised below:

i) *The Assembly of the Union* is the supreme organ of the Union and is composed of Heads of State and Government or their duly accredited representatives. The powers and functions of the assembly are elaborated in its Rules of Procedures. In Rules 4(e) to (g), for example, the Assembly's powers and functions include deciding on intervention in, and determining sanctions to be imposed on a Member State. Whereas in Article 9(1)(e), the Assembly can monitor the implementation of the Union's decisions and ensure compliance by the Member States, Rule 4(1)(b) provides that this can be done 'through appropriate mechanisms'. According to Rules 33 and 34, the decisions of the Assembly fall into three categories – namely: (a) regulations; (b) directives; and (c) recommendations, declarations, resolutions and opinions. Regulations and directives are binding on Member States, whereas recommendations, declarations, resolutions and opinions, by contrast, are not binding. a) In general, the Assembly is mandated to determine the common policies of the Union, establish its priorities and adopt its annual programme; b) monitor the implementation of policies and decisions of the Union as well as ensure compliance by all Member States through appropriate mechanisms; c) accelerate the political and socioeconomic integration of the continent; d) give directives to the Executive Council, the PSC or the Commission on the management of conflicts, wars, acts of terrorism, emergency situations and the restoration of peace (AU 2015). It also appoints the chairman of the Commission and his or her deputy or deputies and commissioners of the Commission and determines their functions and terms of office. It also appoints and terminates the appointment of the judges of the Court of Justice and adopts the budget of the Union; it determines the AU's policies, establishes its priorities, adopts its annual programme and monitors the implementation of its policies and decisions.

ii) *The Executive Council* is composed of ministers or authorities designated by the governments of Member States. It is tasked with the responsibility of preparing the sessions of the Assembly and determining the issues to be submitted for decisions. It also promotes cooperation and coordination with the Regional Economic Communities (RECs), the African Development Bank (AFDB) and other African institutions and the United Nations Economic Commission for Africa (UNECA). In performing these functions, it also determines the policies for cooperation between the AU and Africa's partners, considers and makes recommendations to the Assembly on the Commission's structure, functions and statutes and ensures the promotion of gender equality in all AU programmes (AU 2015). While the Assembly is the highest decision-making body of the AU, the Council is also empowered to coordinate and take decisions on policies in areas of common interest to Member States. Under Article 13, these areas of common interest to the Member States include foreign trade; energy, industry and mineral resources; food, agriculture and animal resources, livestock production and forestry; water resources and irrigation; environmental protection, humanitarian action and disaster response and relief; transport and communications; insurance; education, culture, health and human resources development; science and technology; nationality, residency and immigration matters amongst others. These encompass practically all the issues that the Union is seized with. In effect, both the Assembly and the Executive Council appear to be co-decision-making bodies. However, in practice, the Assembly makes all principal decisions because the decisions of the Council are subject to its endorsement or approval before they can take effect.

iii) *The Pan African Parliament (PAP)* as an organ of the AU is constituted according to Articles 5 and 17 of the Constitutive Act. Though contemplated as one of the organs of the AEC according to the 1991

Abuja Treaty, it was only inaugurated in March 2004. It aims to evolve into an institution with full legislative powers, whose members are elected by universal adult suffrage. At present, it exercises advisory and consultative powers and currently has 230 members. PAP representatives are elected by the legislatures of their Member State, rather than being elected directly by the people. According to Article 8 of the 2014 Protocol of the PAP, it is meant to serve as the legislative organ of the AU, receiving a determination from the assembly on subjects or areas in which it may propose draft model laws, though it may on its own make proposals on the subject/areas in which it may submit or recommend draft model laws to the Assembly for its consideration and approval. According to paragraph 2, of Article 8, the PAP can also request the attendance of officials of the other organs of the AU at its sessions to offer it assistance in the discharge of its duties; promote the programmes and objectives of AU in Member States; receive, consider and submit opinions on draft legal instruments, treaties and other international agreements as may be referred to it by the Council or Assembly and liaise with National Parliaments or other deliberative bodies and the Parliaments of the RECs on all matters relating to the AU and regional integration in Africa.

According to Article 3 of its protocol, it aims to (a) give a voice to the African peoples and the diaspora; (b) facilitate the effective implementation of the policies and objectives of the AU; (c) promote the principles of human and peoples' rights and democracy in Africa; (d) encourage good governance, respect for the rule of law, transparency and accountability in Member States; e) promote peace, security and stability, f) strengthen continental solidarity, cooperation and development, and build a sense of common destiny and facilitate cooperation among RECs in Africa and their Parliamentary fora. One of its key other functions is to encourage National and Regional Parliaments to ratify and integrate treaties adopted by the AU into their legal systems (AU 2015).

iv) *The African Court on Human and Peoples' Rights* is a continental court established by African countries to ensure protection of human and peoples' rights in Africa. It complements and reinforces the functions of the African Commission on Human and Peoples' Rights. It was established following Article 1 of the Protocol to the African Charter on Human and Peoples' Rights on the establishment of an African Court on Human and Peoples' Rights, (the Protocol) which was adopted by the Member States of the then OAU in Ouagadougou, Burkina Faso, in June 1998. The Protocol came into force on 25 January 2004 after it was ratified by more than 15 countries. It has currently been ratified by only

26 of the 54 Member States of the AU. The court has jurisdiction over all cases and disputes submitted to it concerning the interpretation and application of the African Charter on Human and Peoples' Rights (the Charter), the Protocol, and any other relevant human rights instrument ratified by the states concerned. It consequently has a focus on the promotion of human rights and not on the interpretation nor enforcement of the treaties of the AU.

v) *The Permanent Representatives' Committee (PRC)* is composed of permanent representatives of Member States accredited to the AU and other duly accredited plenipotentiaries of Member States resident at the headquarters of the AU. It is established under Article 21 of the Constitutive Act. Its powers and functions include the following: (a) to act as a liaison between Member States and the Commission; (b) to exercise oversight over the Commission; (c) to facilitate and support the Executive Council in executing its powers and functions; and, (d) to participate in the preparation of the AU's programme of activities (AU 2015). It prepares the work of the Executive Council and acts as its advisory body. It plays a key role in facilitating communication between the AU Commission and the capitals of Member States. It also considers the programme and budget of the Union as well as administrative, budgetary and financial matters of the Commission, and make recommendations to the Executive Council. It also considers matters relating to the programmes and projects of the Union, particularly issues relating to the socioeconomic development and integration of the continent, and make recommendations thereon to the Executive Council. It can thus be considered the critical linkage established between the AU and its Member States and the channel through which the Member State governments participate in the running of the AUC.

vi) *The Specialised Technical Committees (STCs)*: Article 14 of the AU Constitutive Act provides for the establishment of STCs across a range of thematic areas. These STCs are responsible to the Executive Council and are organs of the AU in accordance with Article 5 of the AU Constitutive Act. The process of operationalising the STCs has been ongoing and, as of 1 September 2014, the functions of some STCs were being carried out by various sectorial ministerial conferences.[1] The objective of these committees will be to prepare projects and programmes for the Union and submit them to the Executive Council. STCs are also to ensure their supervision and follow-up on the implementation of decisions taken by the Organs of the Union. They are also meant to ensure the coordination and harmonisation of the projects and programmes of the AU and to submit to the Executive

Council (either on their own initiative or at the request of the Executive Council) reports and recommendations on the implementation of the provisions of the Constitutive Act. The Constitutive Act initially provided for seven STCs but at its February 2009 summit meeting, the Assembly enlarged this number to 14 to make their structure and thematic focus consistent with AU Commission portfolios (see Decision Assembly/AU/Dec.227 (XII) adopted in February 2009 in Addis Ababa, Ethiopia).

vii) *The AU Commission*: The Commission is the key organ playing a central role in the day-to-day management of the AU. Among others, it represents the Union and defends its interests; elaborates draft common positions of the Union; prepares strategic plans and studies for the consideration of the Executive Council; elaborates, promotes, coordinates and harmonises the programmes and policies of the Union with those of the RECs; ensures the mainstreaming of gender in all programmes and activities of the Union. The Commission is mandated, among other functions, in Article 3(2) to: Represent the Union and defend its interests under the guidance of, and as mandated by, the Assembly and the Executive Council; initiate proposals for consideration by other organs; Implement the decisions taken by other organs; Coordinate and monitor the implementation of the decisions of the Union in close collaboration with the PRC and report regularly to the Executive Council; Work out draft common positions of the Union and coordinate the actions of Member States in international negotiations; and, prepare the Union's Programme and budget for approval by policy Organs.

When one looks at these institutions that have been foreseen and in some cases created to drive Africa's integration, the first question that comes to mind is their appropriateness and the choice of the selected institutions. While similar institutions have been adopted in other contexts and geographical instances, it is important to ask whether these institutions are suitable for Africa's context and realities. In this regard there are two perspectives that can be upheld, the one looks at these institutions are standards that are expected to drive the values that such institutions incarnate, and hence they are being set up as aspirations for where the continent aspires to be in a couple of decades down along the line of the integration journey. The contrasting view would be the neofunctionalist expectation that these institutions have actually been set up to function and functionally drive the integration agenda through their daily conduct of business. In the case of Africa, it is likely that the truth lies somewhere in the middle of these two possibilities, hence the process of institutional setup is both aspirational and progressive. Seen from this perspective, institutions are first created and then resources, and efforts are dedicated to make them functional, become and stay relevant and operate efficiently.

Take, for example, the case of the PAP, it was only inaugurated in 2004 and the protocol for its functioning was ratified in 2014, but it is very far from operating as the legislative arm of the AU integration project, because it lacks the means and capacity to hold African Heads of Governments and Executives accountable. It currently only plays an advisory role within the architecture of the organs of the Union. However, for the AU to take more than two decades to set up an institution like the continental parliament, which is supposed to play a key role in driving the integration process is surely problematic for a continent waiting to reap the development benefits of its integration in better governance and improved welfare. This has also been the fate of the Court of Justice and of the financial institutions (African Central Bank and African Monetary Fund to do some of what the IMF and World Bank are currently doing at the moment) also foreseen in Article 5 of the Constitutive Act of the AU, which though identified as important components of the integration project have not yet been fully set up. This raises the question of the amount of thought that actually went into the choice of institutions retained to drive the integration process of the continent.

However, an appropriate institutional framework and infrastructure are the bedrocks upon which development at all levels – local, national, regional and continental is built. Without certainty about the appropriateness of designated institutions, endeavouring to set up and make them functional can be an exercise in futility. How does an institution get to be funded adequately and organised to function optimally if its mandate is only vaguely defined. The question of adequacy and source of funding is critical to the ownership of the integration agenda by the AU Member States and addresses the more fundamental question of the form orientation and integration vision currently being pursued by the AU. Seeking to resolve the question of funding without addressing the more fundamental questions surrounding the vision, the desired destination and road map (including the most suitable institutions to accompany the process) towards the accomplishment of the same may not prove a very fruitful exercise. This question of the funding and the functioning of the AU's institutions of integration (as a collective) is an important one because it also partly explains the little progress registered from 1963 when the OAU was formed and the manner in which the continent's integration agenda is currently being advanced.

Resolving the question of creating appropriate institutions to manage and drive Africa's integration should therefore be considered an important priority. Unfortunately, the Constitutive Act of the AU is limited in this regard in that it does not specify what steps need to be taken to accelerate the political and economic integration of Africa. Neither does it provide clear and sufficient guidance as to the powers and functions of the various organs, institutions and key players, nor the relations among them. Also, it does not contain an institutionalised mechanism for the promotion and management of Union affairs at a national level. No provision is made in the Act for remedying or rectifying the prevailing and dominant intergovernmental tendencies carried over from the OAU, except by stating, in Article 33, that the Act shall replace the Charter of the OAU (OAU 2000). For the institutions of the AU to deliver on their mandate of driving the integration process, they need to be clearly given this mandate and the accompanying authority and resources to do so. But this has not been the case up to now because the question of sovereignty pooling and sovereignty transfer was never seriously considered during the formation of the OAU or the transition from the OAU to the AU. There seems to be a long-standing reluctance to create and empower supranational institutions that are well-resourced and mandated to manage Africa's integration process. Even with the creation of the AU, the Member States do not yet seem ready to empower the continental institutions with supranational responsibilities over the integration process.

In a 2001 report of the secretary general on the implementation of the Lusaka Summit on the texts relating to the key organs of the AU and as part of the management of the transition from the OAU to the AU, it was recommended in paragraphs (f) and (g) on the powers of the Assembly that it be called upon to facilitate the progressive pooling of the sovereignty of Member States to be exercised by the Commission in the interest of the Union and to determine areas in which Member States can entrust the Union with the responsibility of promoting their collective interests (OAU 2001). But these recommendations never made it through to the rules and procedures governing the actual functioning of the General Assembly. In a similar vein in paragraph 5, Article 8 of the protocol of the PAP, the functions of the PAP are only limited to those allocated to it by the Assembly and the Council, but the range of discretional activities allocated to it in paragraph 2 and 3 of the same Article 8 do not extend to the assembly and council. This essentially means that the PAP cannot institute an enquiry into the conduct of the assembly, court and council or their members. The Assembly of Heads of States currently remains the sole organ upon which all decisions reside; it is answerable to itself, not subject to scrutiny by any other organ and allows no other organ to drive the integration agenda beyond the mandate it has expressly delegated to them. This makes the AU and its institutions a model of intergovernmental cooperation governed by an Assembly of Heads of States whose activities are managed by a sort of secretariat called the AU Commission, which is in sharp contrast with the EU experience, as examined in the next section.

THE FUNCTIONING OF EUROPE'S INSTITUTIONS OF INTEGRATION

The EU and its integration experience continue to occupy a central place in the broader discussion on regionalism and the approach to regional integration. In public and policy debates, generic references are made to the EU's institutional setup (characterised by a mix of supranational and intergovernmental institutions. In some cases, reference is made to the centrality of trade and the establishment of a common market. For others, by contrast, it is the social dimension (the so-called European social model) that has characterised European integration. For security specialists, instead, the European experience of integration has been characterised by the presence of external threats and the role of the transatlantic alliance in fostering further integration, in particular during the Cold War (Deutsch 1968). Those looking at the nuts and bolts of the actual policy convergence of the European polity would probably emphasise the gradualist approach endorsed by Jean Monnet, the principal architect of the early European integration, which has then become a key feature of the neofunctionalist school (Haas 1958). Federalists would, on their part, underline the role of charismatic and devoted leaders (Riker 1964), while liberal intergovernmentalists would argue that the integration of Europe was nothing else than a rational and self-interested bargain among governments, underpinned by clear economic incentives (Moravcsik 1993).

Europe's experience in the creation of institutions of integration dates back to the post–World War II (WWII) era with the creation of the Organization for European Economic Cooperation (OEEC). The OEEC was founded in 1948 to administer the US Marshall Plan to reconstruct post-war Europe. In the creation of the OEEC, Europe sought to avoid Fascism, Nazism as well as nationalist protectionism, while establishing peace and prosperity through trade links. These aspirations gave rise to nascent forms of supranational institutional development through the promotion of progressive integration in strategic key sectors. The Schuman Plan (1950) foresaw limited sectoral integration but on a supranational basis to place the war-triggering sectors of coal and steel under the auspices of one authority, the so-called 'High Authority' (Gilbert 2012: 9). It was an explicitly political proposal but followed a functional approach of economic integration though with wider political objectives. Following that, the Treaty of Paris (1951) ushered in the formation of the European Coal and Steel Community (ECSC) (formally founded in 1952) to realise a common market for coal, steel and iron ore for the six-member countries, the then West Germany, France, Italy, Belgium, the Netherlands and Luxembourg. By the time the Treaty of Rome was adopted in 1957 to formalise the creation of the European Economic

Community, these six countries had over five years of supranational coordination in the management of shared resources. Learning from this early experience, the founding nations of European integration agreed to the creation of a number of institutions that would play both a supranational and intergovernmental role. There were five such key institutions that served as the foundation and building block of the EU's institutional development. These included (i) the Council of the EU, (ii) the European Council, (iii) the European Commission, (iv) The European Parliament (EP) and (v) the EU Court of Justice.

These five major institutions, their nature and functions can be summarised in table 4.2.

As can be gathered from the table, Europe's institutions are made up of a combination of supranational and intergovernmental hybrid models of governance. The Commission, for example, is a supranational organisation while the Council is generally an intergovernmental forum. In allocating responsibilities to European-level institutions, the EU made use of the principle of 'subsidiarity' (a guiding principle within the EU to ensure that institutions do not take on responsibilities that national and sub-national governments can do better). This has been the principle followed to determine the distribution of competencies between national governments and European-level institutions. It was instituted in the Treaty of Amsterdam to ensure that decisions in areas that do not fall under the EU's exclusive competencies (such as health care and education) should remain at the national level (Ginsberg 2010: 143). Where competencies remain with the EU, it is guided by the principle of 'proportionality' according to which the content or form of the action taken by the EU must not exceed what is necessary to achieve the objective of the treaty. As such it can be argued that 'the pendulum of European integration swings between Member States, who retain and delegate sovereignty, and EU bodies, who cultivate their scope for agency' (Ginsberg 2010: 144). This functions as a principal–agent relationship in which one is mandated to act on behalf of the other along the lines of mutually agreed principles with delegated and shared responsibilities.

Overall the EU's governmental system as a body seems closer to a parliamentary system where legislators from the EP hold accountable the political appointees in the executive represented by the Commission. The Commission is thus answerable to the EP, which has a supervisory role vis-à-vis the Commission. By subjecting a supranational executive to an elected parliament, the EU has established a constitutional system of checks and balances where Commissioners attend EP sessions to reply to queries by MEPs and sometimes have to justify chosen policies (Ginsberg 2010: 148). This has created a mix of institutions driving the integration process in ways that go beyond the mere execution of their individual contemplated mandate. As such the EU

Table 4.2 Functions and Nature of Europe's Five Major Regional Institutions

Institution/Nature and Date of Origin	*Major Functions*	*Governance/Voting Mechanism/and Sample Action*
Commission (1952) Supranational Executive and bureaucracy	Guards/enforces treaty and oversees daily EU functioning. Represents EU abroad and negotiates, initiates/executes legislation and budget. Issues reports, studies, regulations and directives. Oversees transposition of EU laws into national legislation. Manages the EU's competition policy.	Simple majority. Charged to bring to the European Court of Justice any member governments that fail to comply with treaty law, for example by not transposing EU agreements into national legislation within a reasonable time.
Council (1952) Intergovernmental Executive and Legislator	It co-legislates with EP; decides policy in areas of security and defence; Approves budget with EP; asks the Commission to conduct studies and submit proposals. Council has the power to pass European Laws, coordinate the general economic policies of the Member States in the context of the Economic and Monetary Union (EMU), to approve the EU budget jointly with the European Parliament and to conclude international agreements between the EU and other countries or international organisations. It also takes decisions pertaining to Common Foreign and Security Policies (CFSP) and measures pertaining to police and judicial cooperation in criminal matters.	Unanimity, consensus, qualified majority voting (QMV). Constructive abstention. Enhanced cooperation.
European Parliament (1952) Transnational co-legislator	Co-legislates with council, oversees EU bodies and approves budget together with council; approves enlargement/associations; Confirms/censures commission. Asks the commission to conduct studies/submit proposals and adopt reports.	Simple or absolute majority.
Court of Justice Supranational court	Interprets treaties. Rules on treaty law. Ensures uniformity of EC Law.	Simple majority.

(*continued*)

Table 4.2 (Continued)

Institution/Nature and Date of Origin	*Major Functions*	*Governance/Voting Mechanism/and Sample Action*
European Council Intergovernmental summit of Heads of Government/ States Plus council and commission presidents and higher representative	Sets broad guidelines, makes overarching decisions, offers strategic direction and impetus; breaks logjams. Delegates powers to EU bodies to reduce transaction costs. Nominates, appoints Commission and Commission President, Council Secretary General, High Representative, and Executive Board/President of the ECB.	Consensus. QMV on the selection of European Council and Commission Presidents and on the appointment of a new commission.

Source: Compiled from Ginsberg (2010).

institutions have become leaders of integration in their own right (Laursen 2003).

There are a number of factors that can explain the relative success of Europe in creating institutions to promote integration. A major consideration is the fact that the initial six countries involved in the integration process approached the process with experience and history in building other institutions of regional governance. Another critical lesson from the construction of Europe's institutions of integration is the careful attention given to the management of the sovereignty concerns of Member States. Responsibilities have been carefully handed over to supranational institutions and principles (like subsidiarity and proportionality) outlined for these institutions to ensure that they're not a replacement for Member States but only an enhancer of effective cooperation. Sovereignty concerns are treated as legitimate by the Member States and their expectations are carefully managed along the process of further integration.

CONCLUSION

The way Africa's integration has evolved, and its institutions set up to function may explain the lack of implementation of some of its commitments towards regional integration. The fact that some institutions have been foreseen but not yet set up or most set-up institutions do not demonstrate the kind of functional efficiency that they demonstrate in other instances (like in the EU) is problematic. It may suggest that not much critical thought was invested into the choice of institutions and that even less effort is being invested to ensure their functional efficiency talk less of their being endowed with the financial resources and legal capabilities to drive the integration agenda as is expected of them. Commenting on the performance of Africa's institutions of integration, the funding and functioning in this manner without comparing it against another model would not have given sufficient context. In this regard, the EU's institutions of integration in their combined supranational and intergovernmental character serve as a standard against which Africa's institutions can be judged. In this regard, the EU and its institutions of integration serve as a good comparative template against which to contemplate the setup and functioning of Africa's own institutions of integration. The neofunctionalism underpinnings of Europe's institutions provide the driving force behind the role institutions are expected to play in promoting integration. Particularly the notion of task expansion and spillover (tendency of regional groups to expand the scope of issues areas and to move from cooperation in 'low politics' to cooperation in high politics seems to capture the notion that capacity is built and acquired through the experience of being part of the integration process and this strengthens the regional institution's agency and capacity to drive the integration agenda. This, sort of explains what Africa's experience with its institutions of integration has been. However, sovereignty pooling and transfer, including empowering created supranational institutions contribute to strengthen regional institutions as they play a critical coordination role in promoting integration. This has been recognised as important for Africa's integration, as mentioned earlier during the transition from the OAU to the AU, but its materialisation is still to be effected in the setup and functioning of its current institutions. Given this context, it is important that steps be undertaken to make these institutions more fit for purpose and empowered to drive Africa's integration. A good starting place would be to encourage their adoption of a different paradigm of integration altogether, including adopting a developmental regionalism approach to integration, as the next chapter argues.

NOTE

1. See more at: http://www.au.int/en/organs/stc#sthash.cmW3nw8p.dpuf

Chapter 5

A Case for Developmental Regionalism in Africa's Integration

INTRODUCTION

As examined in the previous chapter, Africa's integration trajectory has been quite unique and the subject of a lot of debate. It has been customary to interpret the outcome of its integration objectives through the lens of assumptions about the models that it may be following. From all indications, Africa is arguably guided by the linear integration framework especially if one looks at the objectives that have been built into the Abuja Treaty of 1991 establishing the African Economic Community (AEC). The steps that it commits to undertake towards the attainment of a common market remain up to this moment the underlying goal and objective of its integration endeavours. There have been adjustments along the way from the time of the creation of the OAU to today, including during the establishment of the African Union in 2001, including the creation of the New Partnership for Africa's Development (NEPAD). The switch from the political objective of liberation and the fight against apartheid of the 1960s to the economics and market integration objectives of the 1990s together have constituted the backbone and pillars of Africa's integration project. This chapter like the rest of this volume intends to make the case for a change of paradigm in Africa's approach to integration. Drawing heavily on a key characteristic of European Integration, it attempts to make the argument that this change of paradigm would come principally through the adoption of an evidence-based approach to the promotion and fostering of integration. Associated with this evidence-based approach is the articulation of the benefits of integration and its distribution. Taken together, these two components (evidence and benefits distribution) ought to be the cornerstones of the proposed change of paradigm towards the adoption of developmental regionalism. Developmental regionalism in itself is explored as a concept that could be beneficial if applied in the context of African integration. Accordingly, the chapter will be further divided into four subsections: the first section will make a brief case for the adoption of an evidence-based approach to integration in Africa, while the next section puts forward 'A Case for the Adoption of Developmental Regionalism in Africa's Integration Practice'. The third section will describe the developmental regionalism paradigm and the benefits of its adoption in the case of Africa's integration, while the final section will summarise and conclude the chapter.

THE IMPERATIVE OF EVIDENCE-DRIVE INTEGRATION IN AFRICA

As already noted, the Lagos Plan of Action and the Abuja Treaty establishing the AEC spelt out the economic, political and institutional mechanisms for attaining the objectives of African integration while NEPAD was conceived as a development framework for the region (UNECA 2004: 1). As is now customary with Africa's approach to its integration, the theme that cuts across its integration programs and policies is the underlying philosophy of collective action through cooperation and/or integration to attain objectives that are 'perceived' or expected to accumulate certain developmental benefits for the African Union and its Member States. However, the one consistently missing element with each of these programs and their benefits is any documented evidence of the proposed or promised benefits of the integration project. This has made ownership and adoption of the integration agenda a challenge for these African countries, because the benefits to be accrued from integration are not clearly spelt out as has been the case in other integration arrangements like the European Union's.

In a sense, the continent's commitment to integration has been driven by loyalty to Nkrumah and the founding fathers of African unity who professed their firm belief that a united Africa (economically integrated into a larger market and politically coordinated in Nkrumah's view as a federated union) stood a better chance at influencing the course of its development and the nature of its engagement with the rest of the world. In the minds of Nkrumah and the founding fathers of Africa's integration project, they argued that if Africa's multiple resources were used for its own development, the continent would be among the most modernised in the world (Nkrumah 1965: 2). Such an outcome is desirable if it can be accomplished but its mere articulation fails to take into account the standard resource curse argument and the political economy of natural resources ownership and exploitation in Africa. This makes the desirable very difficult to achieve when the incentives and right conditions are not assembled. There was no question at the time whether such aspirations were desirable and in all likelihood, the euphoria of the post-independence years and the formal end of colonisation probably blocked out of the minds of these newfound African states the feasibility of these cooperation aspirations within a fast-paced globalisation era.

For starters, the bulk of the trade and economic relations between African countries at the time were with their former colonial masters and the bulk of the economic infrastructure in the form of agro-industrial plantations had been created to serve the markets in the North and not necessarily with the intentions of structuring these newly independent African economies. This has meant the predominance of North–South trade relations which has persisted up to today, notwithstanding the very many laudable efforts to increase intra-African trade. This North–South Trade is happening for countries with geographical proximity that however have little to trade with each other but nonetheless aspire towards the creation of a large common market that will make them globally competitive. It goes without saying that there has to be a significant alteration in the trade relations amongst African countries and perhaps a redress in their trade balances with their Northern Trade partners, particularly with respect to the value addition in trade exchanges and upward movements in global value chains. This would bring to centre stage the question of beneficiation of minerals as opposed to exporting them in their raw state as well as the processing of agricultural products that could constitute the basis for Africa's industrialisation as shall be discussed in more detail in the next chapter. Beneficiation and value addition in agricultural production together with investments in forward and backward linkages could constitute the basis for an industrialisation project that would make for both economic transformation and development. This can be mainstreamed and pursued as a collective objective within Africa's integration project and this change of approach would constitute in itself a change in paradigm that could be qualified as the adoption of a developmental regionalism paradigm.

The aspirations of cooperation for global relevance and its importance remain noble and relevant but there are still many challenges to be overcome for actual effective cooperation amongst African countries. The critical question that needs to be asked in this regard, is what it would take for African countries to collaborate with each other in a manner that will make their joint pursuit of developmental objectives a reality? What does such a cooperation look like and under what conditions would it be fulfilled? The answers to these questions merit exclusive and elaborate volumes, but for the purposes of this chapter and section, it is suggested that the adoption of *evidence-based policy*making in the area of regional integration and a *delineation of the benefits* associated with integration could be two good starting points and important elements along this journey of making integration more successful in Africa. This is supported by the experience of earlier regional economic integration arrangements in certain regions in Africa and Latin America that reveals that sovereign nations only agree to be a committed part of any regional integration/developmental efforts when some minimal conditions are met, including:

i) Expectations that there will be benefits for each member, in terms of increased trade, investment and industrial productivity.
ii) There will be an equitable distribution of such benefits across the participating members.
iii) Efforts towards developmental regionalism will only be successful when the Member States have the national capabilities necessary to overcome the obstacles to regional cooperation.

This tripartite elements of '*expected benefits*', '*distribution of benefits*' and '*national capabilities*' hold the key to Africa's successful regional integration effort. The determination of the expected benefits can become critical knowledge that will drive the deepening of the integration project and also make it possible to ascertain the losers and winners in order to designate and implement a compensation scheme as part of efforts to distribute the benefits by finding ways of compensating the losers from the integration project. The setup of social cohesion funds and the adoption of revenue redistribution mechanisms to compensate losers in deepening integration projects have proven to be instrumental in advancing regional integration projects. These mechanisms are well documented within Europe's integration experience as well as the practice of clearly delineating the expected benefits of integration. This is one other thing that Africa's integration project could learn from the integration experience of the European Union. With respect to the enactment of evidence-based integration policies, there was a study commissioned to ascertain the costs of non-integration in Europe in 1988 and it produced what has become known as the 'Cecchini report'. Below is a paragraph that is an excerpt of the Cecchini report as presented to the Member States of the European Union:[1]

> The Commission today revealed the results of a major study which it commissioned to evaluate scientifically the benefits of the single market. This study which will shortly be published in book form provides the hard evidence, the confirmation of what those
>
> Who are engaged in building Europe have always known: that the failure to achieve a single market has been costing European Industry dearly in *unnecessary costs* and *lost opportunities*.

> That the completion of the internal market will provide the economic context for the regeneration of European industry in both goods and services; and that it will give a permanent boost to the prosperity of the people of Europe.
>
> The study not only quantifies the heavy cost that we now pay because of the many barriers which fragment the Community's economy into twelve separate markets; It also calculates the value of the immense opportunities which the completion of the internal market will open up: opportunities for growth, for Job creation, for economies of scale, for improved productivity and profitability, for healthier competition, for professional and business mobility, for stable prices and for consumer choice.
>
> The total potential economic gain to the Community as a whole is estimated to be in the region of ECU 200 billion or more expressed in 1988 prices. This would add about 5% to the Community's Gross Domestic Product.

Such evidence-based policymaking can prove critical for the advancement of the integration agenda to the extent that it gives stakeholders and actors the kind of substantive information that they need to lobby their constituencies in favour of the proposed integration agenda. There is a lot that can be said about just this extract from the Cecchini report. Going by a simple sequencing of events, it is worth noting that the presentation of this report in 1988 can be used as a litmus test of the mood in Europe at the time. Following this report and in 1991, European leaders met in the city of Maastricht in the Netherlands and started negotiations on what would later become the Treaty of Maastricht of 1992 establishing the European Union.

The Maastricht Treaty in its Preamble made the increase in the standards of living of the European population one of the key objectives of the regionalisation process. Article 2 of the treaty includes a high level of employment and social protection as well as raising the standards of living and quality of life, while articles 48 to 51 encourage free mobility of labour among EU Member States accompanied by a commensurate aggregation of social-insurance benefits. Subsequent articles of the same treaty encourage coordination of efforts in the fields of education and vocational training and the mutual recognition of diplomas and other certificates of formal education. These are legal provisions that make for deeper levels of integration of participating countries in areas as detailed as standardisation of educational qualifications and labour market practices. These are not expressed as desirable outcomes but as *legally enforceable* terms of treaties that participating Member States sign up to, which in so many ways is unlike Africa's integration experience.

The provisions of the Maastricht Treaty came on the back of earlier provisions contained in the Rome Treaty that had enshrined the notion of social protection for European Citizens within their integration agenda and processes. The basic idea behind Europe's social approach to integration is the notion that economic and social progress ought to evolve together and economic growth combined with social cohesion (Jepsen and Pascual 2005: 234). It was also within the Maastricht Treaty that EU Member States relinquished their rights to the individual use of their monetary policy and committed to a coordinated use of their fiscal policies. Having established a European Central Bank (ECB) earlier; these provisions paved the way for the eventual adoption of a single currency, the Euro, by a majority of Member States. The adoption of the Euro in January 1999 implied the completion of the Economic and Monetary Union (EMU) and a major step towards the completion of the Single European Market (SEM), giving up their economic and monetary sovereignty and adopting a common currency as per initial agreement of the early six EEC members at The Hague in 1969.

In the examination of the earlier episodes that defined the milestones of African regionalism and contrary to the experiences highlighted as far as Europe is concerned above, there is surely a need for the prioritisation of evidence-based decision-making. By evidence-based decision-making, we mean the theoretical conceptualisation and empirical demonstration of the benefits of further and deepened integration, or the absence thereof as was done in Europe. On the contrary, Africa's integration seems to be riding exclusively on the ideological attachment to the notion of Pan-Africanism (the desire to unite black and oppressed people from across the globe and sell to them the advantages of cooperating together for collective self-reliance and upliftment mostly as a response to their shared collective past of operation and a resolve to find a better place for themselves in the global world order). While there may be nothing intrinsically wrong with the pursuit of cooperation on this basis (people with a similar identity and past coming together to promote their collective upliftment), it is however not a sufficient motivation to translate into the identification of suitable policies and approaches to cooperation, especially when dealing with countervailing stronger forces of national identities and the newly acquired status of nation states within the community of nations. The advantages of economic cooperation and integration are hardly in dispute though the underlying arguments and logic may be contested and challenged especially in the context and experience of Africa. There is however hardly any dispute that no matter what approach any region settles and options it decides to pursue for its integration, it should be able to clearly demonstrate through indisputable evidence the real anticipated consequences of the choices they profess as well as the anticipated benefits of the same.

In addition, any regional integration arrangement that is incapable of ascertaining the promised benefits of its proposed integration would also struggle to have an effective and meaningful conversation about the distribution of these benefits. It should be easy to calculate, for example, the costs to businesses and loss of welfare accumulated by administrative procedures at border posts and be able to translate that into actual loss in welfare gains to the community as a prelude to making the case for a borderless engagement between countries. The process should go from the prediction of theory to the empirical testing for evidence, taking into account the contextual reality of specific geographical regions. The assumptions of theoretical predictions may not always capture the contextual realities in developing countries. therefore when such predictions are tested on the contextual realities of some countries, the results make it possible empirical testing of these predictions to falsify their prediction. whereas when empirical testing validates theoretical predictions it makes evidence-based policymaking possible. It is often assumed within the theoretical literature that economic integration, especially amongst developing countries offers an impressive list of benefits or economic payoffs to help accelerate modernisation. According to Sloan (1971), these are some of the theorised benefits of integration:

i) Integration can serve as a means for the attainment of economies of scale. This is important because for every type of industrial production, the question of the optimum market size arises. This implies that unless the volume of sales reaches a certain minimum, cost per unit and the price the consumer will be high and the capacity to compete low (Sloan 1971: 144). The argument is that production costs decline steadily as output increases and consequently large market outlets are indispensable, particularly if one needs to take advantage of certain production methods. This argument however may not be applicable to the production and trade of agricultural products or natural resources that are the principal export commodities of most developing countries. It also does not factor in the changing nature of global trade or make the argument while such economies of scale are best achieved within economic integration governed by geographical proximity as opposed to access of the same production markets to global markets.
ii) The advantage of more specialisation is the second benefit of economic integration. The main rationale for economic integration from this viewpoint is that larger markets are superior to smaller markets from the point of view of factor efficiency. Once assured of a larger market beyond the national borders, new plants may be located in countries where particular products can be produced more efficiently.
iii) The third benefit promised by economic integration is that through competition; it would serve as a means of enhancing efficiency in industry. It is hoped that the wider markets provided by regional economic integration would help to overcome the problems caused by inefficient production methods through gradually increased competition.

iv) The fourth benefit promised by economic integration is that it will serve as a means of reducing the external vulnerability of developing economies. It is hoped it will improve their foreign-exchange earning capacities by first enabling them to export manufactured goods and eventually capital goods to their neighbours. The beneficiaries of developmental regionalism, it is argued, would no longer find themselves almost totally dependent upon the export of one or two primary products to one or two industrialised nations as they will be able to diversify their exports both in kind and with respect to the destination.

v) The fifth expected benefit of economic integration is that it will improve the bargaining power of the regional members with the industrialised countries.

While each of these expected benefits merits a standalone examination, their promises are not completely far-fetched and also the theoretical frameworks underpinning most of these analyses remain the consideration of trade between developed countries, the above-mentioned benefits also have a development flavour by highlighting just a few benefits developing countries stand to benefit from pursuing economic integration.

These are subject off-course to many other factors, but the imperative of contextualising these expectations within developing countries' realities will only be materialised through evidence-based policymaking. Evidence-based policymaking may be difficult to pursue when theoretical models and frameworks/tools have certain ideological assumptions/ideological tint (like the dominance of markets in the capitalist ideology) but choosing to base the adoption of any policy on evidence still remains superior to going by proposals that sound appealing but may not be in sync with approaches adopted by other regional integration arrangements. This emphasis on evidence-based decision-making shall make the measurement and distribution of benefits possible and ought to be the main component of the paradigm shift that becomes the first step towards the adoption of a developmental regionalism approach, which approach is briefly examined in the section that follows.

A CASE FOR THE ADOPTION OF DEVELOPMENTAL REGIONALISM IN AFRICA'S INTEGRATION PRACTICE

According to Davies (1996), the adoption of a 'development integration' approach (developmental regionalism) entails the adoption of both a macro and micro coordination in a multisectoral program embracing production, infrastructure and trade, as well as ensuring a more equitable balance from the benefits of regional integration by complementing efforts towards trade integration by efforts *towards regional industrial development*. Africa's approach towards integration thus far has been heavily biased towards trade and market integration and light on coordination towards regional industrial development, probably because of the weak industrial base of most of its participating Member States. However, their aspiration towards industrialisation has remained alive and as shall be argued in the next chapter; there are still options and possibilities open for the pursuit of industrialisation that ought to create sufficient avenues for regional industrial development cooperation. Adopting this approach to regional cooperation would make the integration project to be more beneficial for all participating countries and would cause Africa's integration to move away from the pure emphasis and focus on the integration of markets which is often a trade liberalisation agenda.

In 2013, a report by the UNCTAD made an argument that African countries needed to adopt an approach to regional integration that embraces the developmental regionalism conceptualisation. It defined 'developmental regionalism' as cooperation among countries in a broader range of areas that could include investment, research and development, as well as policies aimed at accelerating regional industrial development and regional infrastructure provision, such as building up better networks of roads and railway (UNCTAD 2013). According to Sloan (1971), developmental regionalism refers to the joint policies of economic cooperation, coordination and integration among underdeveloped countries designed to accelerate the rate of development of both the Member States and the geographical region. His very early arguments about developmental regionalism were based on the assumption and belief that nations which share a regional identity may be capable of helping one another to develop more rapidly than if each country pursued a solely nationalistic course.

The UNCTAD (2013) report on development in Africa conceptualises the notion of developmental regionalism as a development-based integration agenda that is aimed at securing the traditional benefits of regional integration by ensuring that such benefits flow to all member countries while seeking to enhance their integration into world markets. It proposes an approach that favours a traditional focus on gradual and sequenced trade liberalisation alongside conscious and planned policy actions aimed at building the productive capacities of member countries and promoting industrial restructuring. The agenda extends beyond tariffs and nontariff measures, import and export quotas and bans, technical and phytosanitary standards, to include issues such as competition policy, the provision of infrastructure and other public goods, investment, promotion of research and development and building the domestic productive capacities of both the private sector and state-owned enterprises to ensure the greatest impact and efficiency. Within this framework, the emphasis of developmental regionalism is on facilitating industrial restructuring and economic transformation through the implementation of 'strategic' trade policies that are consistent with the domestic industrial policy frameworks of the states involved. This requires a level of harmonisation and policy coordination that can facilitate joint planning and execution of policy priorities at the regional level in a manner that is being prioritised and implemented at the national level. Also under the UNDP report's proposal of developmental regionalism, 'gradual and sequenced trade liberalisation' is combined with policy actions, such as coordinated investments into regional transport infrastructure, in order to improve linkages between the states involved and enhance the productive capacities of the sub-regions and regions as a whole.

It can thus be argued that developmental regionalism thrives through the promotion of policy harmonisation among participating countries in a regional arrangement and its promotion goes hand in hand with the strengthening of national policy formulation capabilities and related structures, institutions and the implementation capabilities of national governments to design and implement programs from formulated policies (UNCTAD 2013: 97). It is very important to emphasise the fact that policies and plans alone will not deliver the expected developmental results without a commensurate emphasis on developing the capacity and capabilities both domestically and at the regional level to deliver upon the desired objectives. Capacities and capabilities have been a challenge for the African Union and its integration project, whereas it is certainly not beyond the means and resources of 54 African governments to dedicate the kind of resources that is needed for the development of the requisite capacity to intensify cooperation in the other stated areas besides trade liberalisation. It boils down to the creation of the requisite political will and prioritisation of the regional integration projects at the national level. Such prioritisation would be greatly enhanced as earlier argued, if the benefits of integration are clearly spelt out and sufficient evidence generated to demonstrate to the domestic constituencies that they stand to benefit from the regional integration project.

This therefore also implies that for Africa's integration to be truly considered developmental in approach there have to be complementary activities to accompany the trade liberalisation agenda. This is the reason why it is important to adopt and mainstream a developmental regionalism agenda that strengthens the trade integration agenda. Such an augmented agenda could include, for example, cooperation on a bilateral agreement for cross-border infrastructure projects like building a transnational bridge to facilitate and encourage trade while at the same time pursuing harmonisation of systems and laws that would enhance the trade liberalisation agenda through the creation of a customs union (Sloan 1971: 142). To be successful, the African Union would have to adopt the kind of developmental regionalism framework suggested by Adejumobi and Kreiter (2016) which comprises the following six pillars:

i) Building a strong institutional architecture and enhancing capacity to drive the regional integration agenda,
ii) A clear articulation of goals, objectives, essence, nature and direction of the regional integration project, and benefits of regional integration as a mechanism for facilitating regional development,
iii) Ensuring peace and security as a composite and foundation of a regional integration agenda,
iv) Evolving complementary and symmetrical benefits for all Member States involved in the regional development project,
v) Articulation of regional public goods and development priorities necessary for facilitating economic transformation in the region including infrastructure, trade, agriculture and food security, private sector development and industrialisation and
vi) Evolving a bond of common regional citizenship and identity is necessary for regional human capital mobilisation.

Ismail (2018) proposes a similar framework that also contains important ingredients suitable for Africa's developmental regionalism agenda through cooperation in four interrelated areas, including:

i) Cooperation in building mutually beneficial trade integration (fair trade integration),
ii) Cooperation on industrial development and upgrading in regional value chains (transformative industrialisation),
iii) Cooperation on investment in cross-border infrastructure and trade facilitation; and
iv) Cooperation in building democracy, good governance and peace and security.

While each of these elements is being discussed at different fora on the African continent, there is not much evidence suggesting that they have been mainstreamed into the continent's practice of integration. On the continent at the moment, there is not sufficient emphasis on cooperation and integration arrangements that go beyond the attainment of market integration objectives like the creation of a Continental Free Trade Area to facilitate the free movement of goods and people. There is some progress on the movement of goods but lots of restrictions still exist on the free movement of people because of the disparities in levels of economic development between the African countries. However, in regions like Europe, the presence of shared prosperity was a fuel that facilitated the free movement of people and labour through the creation of the Schengen area after the economies had committed to coordinated macroeconomic management, especially monetary policy with the creation of the ECB and the adoption of the Euro as a common currency.

The salient point worth emphasising in the European example is the fact that you cannot pool the risks generated by your respective economies in association with each other without committing to having a say on how each other manages their economy and conduct governance in general. There is, for example, an ideological penchant within the European Union is one of the conditions of ascension for new members to promote the values of a liberal democratic culture that contains a healthy respect for human rights. This is, for example, the reason why a country like Turkey has still not been admitted as a member of the European Union family, despite its geographical proximity and levels of economic development to the Union's. There are some signs of this kind of standardisation of norms and values in the case of the African Union through, for example, a failure to recognise governments that come to power through a military coup, as well as the encouragement to embrace values of good governance through the African Peer Review Mechanism or the MO Ibrahim Leadership Prize for African leaders who handover power and ensure a peaceful democratic transition of power to another government. These incentives however are only coming up at a much later stage in the African Union's own experience of integration and they are at a very early stage of implementation and far away from becoming the standard and norms for institutionalised democratic governance on the continent. In the absence of such shared values in the promotion of good governance and sound macroeconomic management, it will be difficult to have joint planning and policy coordination for coherence as requisites to effective development planning at the regional level. This is the 'sacred cow' (preservation of national sovereignty while desiring cooperation, not integration) of African integration that limits its ability to fully leverage the benefits of its economies working with each other to jointly create and share wealth through integration. This tendency would have to be overcome for Africa to benefit from its pursuit of integration.

The question of shared norms and values in the pursuit of good governance and sound macroeconomic management extends to norms in the ownership and management of Africa's natural resources, which was part of the vision of the founding fathers of African Unity like Kwame Nkrumah. It remains central to the assumed benefits for developmental regionalism and the promises of economic integration. It assumes that expanded markets come with the increasingly efficient use of resources across the reorganised geographic space which is not always the case unless there is a commensurate commitment at the national level being coordinated at the regional level to ensure some kind of shared standards in the approach to managing people and resources (especially on questions of the economy and good governance). This is the way you make participating in integration meaningful and so transform the integrating space to be more globally competitive.

As can be expected, the benefits of developmental regionalism – if delivered – would essentially transform the economies of the members into more integrated and rational regional economies capable of promoting a self-sustaining period of economic growth and shared prosperity, which remains the aspiration of most if not all African countries. Neither increased trade nor increased integration are ends in themselves but the aspiration and ultimate goal remains the prosperity and economic development of nation states who belong to the African regional integration arrangement and this can be enhanced through the adoption of a developmental regionalism paradigm that takes into account all the above-mentioned aspects. While most economies have been concerned with proving or disproving the kinds of benefits which will result from regional economic integration, only a few have analysed the problem of ensuring an equitable distribution of the benefits. However, from a political point of view, this is not a subsidiary issue because nations, be they developed or developing will establish regional cooperative associations only if they expect that the benefits will be divided among them in an equitable manner or at least if they can establish that they stand to benefit from participating than going on by themselves.

The adoption and mainstreaming of a 'developmental regionalism' paradigm would require not only the expansion of the trade liberalisation agenda but also equal efforts invested in the promotion of cooperation on the other identified aspects (production of public goods, development of regional infrastructure projects, coordination of regional industrialisation plans and regional shared norms of macroeconomic management and good governance). It will require that the same effort and energy that has been put into the market integration agenda through the establishment of treaties and legally binding agreements be invested into the broadened or augmented integration agenda that is developmental in flavour and nature. The same energy and emphasis that has been invested in market integration and towards the establishment of an AEC now culminating in the creation of the Continental Free Trade Area would have to be invested in the promotion of developmental regionalism. This would require establishing legally binding treaties, creating and giving the capacity to suitable institutions and mainstreaming these priorities in national and regional/continental programs and agendas.

According to UNCTAD (2013), there are four key 'policy tools and drivers' for fostering developmental regionalism in Africa. The first driver of developmental regionalism is *industrial policy*, which is already being incorporated into regional integration initiatives in Africa through, for example, the regional industrial development policy of the East African Community (EAC) and the industrial development pillar of the Tripartite Free Trade Agreement being negotiated by the EAC, the Common Market for Eastern and Southern Africa (COMESA) and the Southern African Development Community (SADC). The second potential driver of developmental regionalism in Africa is the *use of development corridors*. In theory, these spatial development initiatives encourage intra-regional trade by linking markets. They also improve the productivity of local industries and economies by expanding and improving trade-related infrastructure. The third key policy tool of developmental regionalism is the establishment of *Special Economic Zones (SEZs)*, which can serve both as platforms for supplying regional markets and as locations to source regional inputs and the fourth and final driver is the *promotion of regional value chains*. An approach to regionalism that incorporates these components or even makes them centre stage would require a change in the current emphasis on the trade liberalisation agenda as opposed to treating these components as peripheral to a trade liberalisation agenda.

CONCLUSION

Evidence-based policymaking and intentional discussions around the distributional benefits of regional integration are key ingredients that promote the ownership of any integration agenda as well as enhance its impact on the development of the region and participating Member States. This is contingent upon developing the right capacity to plan and implement development programs as well as upon the political will to incorporate regional priorities in national development plans. In the case of the African Union's practice of regional integration, this would require a change of paradigm in favour of the adoption of a developmental regionalism paradigm that has a few potential components but would certainly succeed once there is a standardisation of shared norms and values in the areas of sound macroeconomic management and the promotion of good democratic governance. The centre-staging of a developmental regionalism agenda would mean encouraging African countries to promote the development of regional value chains by investing in infrastructure and business support services as well as in broader policy areas such as education, innovation and technology. Regional value chains provide local firms with access to foreign markets and inputs, thereby freeing them from the constraints of small domestic markets, and providing them with opportunities to benefit from economies of scale and 'learning-by-doing'. In pursuing these four avenues as a collective, it is expected that developmental regionalism would facilitate industrial restructuring and economic transformation through the implementation of 'strategic' trade policies that are consistent with the domestic industrial policy frameworks of the states involved. As such making developmental regionalism the emphasis and essence of Africa's cooperation could make Member States own the integration agenda and be more engaged and committed to the pursuit of mutual benefits from cooperation. Once the benefits to be accrued from the pursuit of such a developmental regionalism integration agenda is evident to participating Member States, they will not need any further encouragement to own and honour their commitments, which may invariably resolve the implementation challenge of Africa's integration agenda. Making the distinction between a regional integration agenda that has developed as a desired outcome and a developmental regionalism agenda that is pursued as the essence of African cooperation may well hold the key to unravelling the continent's integration and implementation challenges. Seeing that the continent has gone through almost five decades of pursuing several different cooperation initiatives at the continental and sub-regional levels without yielding significant results, it may be just the right time for it to adopt and mainstream developmental regionalism as the principal ideological thrust of its regional integration agenda. Such a change of paradigm would not only affect the trade integration paradigm but could be extended to the continent's approach and practice of industrialisation as shall be briefly explored in the next chapter.

NOTE

1. Excerpt from the Cecchini 1988 report, available online on http://aei.pitt.edu/3813/1/3813.pdf

Chapter 6

Africa's Industrialisation within a Developmental Regionalism Paradigm

INTRODUCTION

Since the late 1990s, Africa has experienced positive economic growth due to improved macroeconomic management, higher domestic demand, and principally, higher commodity prices. Notwithstanding increasing contributions to GDP from manufacturing, financial, telecom and tourism sectors, Africa's economic growth has been mainly driven by primary commodity exports (Morris and Fessehaie 2014: 25). This witnessed high growth has rekindled the debate about how to translate growth to improved standards of living for Africans. Since resources are likely to be depleted at some point in the future and the boom in commodity prices largely driven by the growth of the Chinese economy is not going to last forever, Africa needs to look for ways of diversifying away from the commodity dependence of its economies, and pursuing the structural transformation of its economies. The continent also needs to explore avenues for increasing its global share of trade in manufactured goods and participating at higher levels of Global Value Chains (GVCs). Therefore, it is important for it to revisit the traditional arguments around industrialisation and the role that it can play in economic transformation and the development of the continent and the extent to which the industrialisation objective can be pursued as part of a regional agenda within a developmental regionalism framework.

The combination of high growth, the resources that are generated in the process and the continued developmental challenges still witnessed across the continent has also rekindled the debate around the questions of the structural changes and economic transformation that could come with industrialisation. It remains a common belief (especially backed by the experience, especially of the Newly Industrialized Economies of Asia) that structural change that is often accompanied by industrialisation efforts has proven to be the true pathway to prosperity and significant and meaningful improvements in standards of living. This is because structural change – the shift of resources from low-productivity to high-productivity uses – becomes in this instance the main driver of the witnessed economic growth. This is the kind of growth led by industry (industrialisation) that is desirable for African economies because of the developmental benefit associated with such approaches to economic and societal transformation.

Historically, industry has been the sector that led the process of structural change. Industry contributes to structural change because it is a high-value-added sector into which labour can flow. The average manufacturing–agriculture labour productivity ratio for low-income Africa is 2.5 to 1. Given this very large difference in output per worker and the potential of manufacturing to absorb labour, industrialisation presents a significant opportunity for productivity-enhancing structural change (Ajakaiyea and Page 2012). In addition to this, there are two important structural characteristics related to the types of products produced by the manufacturing sector – diversity and sophistication – that influence productivity change and growth. Cross-country evidence indicates that countries with more diversified production and export structures have higher incomes per capita (Imbs and Wacziarg 2003; Cadot et al. 2011), and countries that produce and export more sophisticated products – those that are primarily manufactured by countries at higher income levels – tend to grow faster (Hausmann et al. 2007; UNIDO 2009).

Thus inclusive and sustainable industrial development is often associated with job creation, sustainable livelihoods, innovation, technology and skills development, food security and equitable growth. Rarely has a country evolved from poor to rich without sustained structural transformation from an agrarian or resource-based economy towards an industrial or service-based economy. This transformation is important to ensure wealth creation through increased economic integration and productivity. This is because by providing decent jobs and by expanding the fiscal revenues needed for social investments, can boost capacity for much-needed inclusive development.

The fact that the benefits of industrialisation are numerous and that it has been the reason why so many countries have been lifted out of underdevelopment justifies its resurgence as an element for important policy consideration on the African integration and development landscape. The questions in these debates have been varied over the years but typically centre around two main axes, being: *Why has Africa not been able to industrialise in spite of the clear benefits of industrialisation and its clear alignment with Africa's developmental aspirations*? This remains a very pertinent question in the case of Africa, especially whenever the experience of the Asian Newly

Industrialized Countries (NICs) is brought into perspective. It is now widely accepted that there was no '*East Asian Model*' of industrialisation per se but that there seemed to have been a specific model for each of the NICs, each having different industrial objectives and using different interventions but within a common context of *export-orientation, good human capital development* and *strong regional spillovers* (Hiley 2000: 58). This meant that each of these economies had a different pattern for industrial and export growth, reliance on foreign direct investment (FDI), technological capability and enterprise structure. They however succeeded in collectively upgrading their industrial production bases and gaining access to global markets through the adoption of export-oriented strategies. Export orientation as a strategy requires global market access and the creation of a competitive advantage in the production of goods. Their experience is informative for Africa because the NICs created a competitive advantage in the production of goods for which they have not always been competitive.

An examination of the experiences of these regions reveal that within the period of 1980s to 2007–2008 the growth of manufacturing in the national share of exports moved significantly East at the detriment of traditionally recognised industrialised economies of the North like Europe and North America. Admittedly, this increase was certainly from a lower base, but it is championed by countries such as the Philippines (59%), Mexico (46%), China (44%), Malaysia (42%) and Thailand (40%). This happened at the same time when traditional industrialised economies were experiencing a decline in their global share of manufacturing Hong Kong (−6%), Japan (−5%), and Sweden, Canada, Germany and Switzerland (all dropping by 2%). One of the reasons why these changes are important for Africa is the realisation that these countries who experienced an increase in their global share of manufacturing are the same countries that in the 1960s would not have been categorised as having a comparative or competitive advantage in manufacturing. This means that the notion of comparative or competitive advantage often touted in much of traditional trade theories may explain the rationale of a production structure given a static or even progressive and dynamic evaluation of countries and their relative resources endowments that bequeath upon them their competitive advantage, but it does not in any way suggest that countries would perpetually retain the comparative or competitive advantages that they once possessed as this is in reality determined by a host of factors outside of the framework and tools of analysis of these trade theoretical frameworks.

The implication for Africa is that its comparative and competitive advantages can be changed just as the NICs have changed theirs. The NICs did not just settle to produce and supply global markets according to their natural endowments, but they created opportunities (a competitive advantage) through carefully crafted/coordinated domestic and regional industrial policies alongside measures that were aimed at building local production capacity. These distinct characteristics of the Asian experience (for individual countries and their collective regional efforts) represent interesting cases for African countries to study. There is no doubt that Africa needs to industrialise so as to provide job opportunities to millions of its young people. This is one sure way the continent can eradicate poverty (like the Chinese have done) while simultaneously facilitating the dynamic processes of technological innovation, skills development, knowledge intensification and capital accumulation (Morris and Fessehaie 2014: 26). Given the consensus that ought to exist around the benefits of industrialisation to Africa, it remains a reality that the continent's many decades of efforts towards industrialisation are not yet yielding the results in Africa that have been recently observed in the NICs. This reality is part of what fuels the renewed interests and debates about the actual obstacles to Africa's industrialisation. This renewed interest is also growing amidst considerations of the opportunities that may exist for Africa's collective industrialisation as part of its regionalisation efforts (developmental regionalism) at the sub-regional and continental levels. To resolve this dilemma, Africa needs to learn concrete lessons from its past attempts at industrialisation, draw lessons from the industrialisation experience of other regions (particularly the NICs in our view) and take cognisance of its current advantages endowments and comparative advantages and the opportunities that are not presented by the changing patterns of global trade to identify and pursue an 'African Unique Pathway' to industrialisation. The opportunities presented by an increase of trade in intermediate goods, that has come with the unbundling and dispersal of global production structures, as well as the increased share of services in global production value chains present are all avenues through which Africa could explore its engagement with industrialisation. To accomplish this, it needs to be able to ask itself the right questions, both at the national as well as the regional level, taking into account the contextual realities of African countries, while reassessing the capacity and potential of regional cooperation and integration to bring about the much desired levels of industrialisation.

Asking the right questions and rightly assessing the available opportunities should lead the African continent towards the most suitable pathway for its industrialisation. This may require developing an understanding of why earlier efforts towards, for example, import-substitution industrialisation, failed, whereas it is known to have been practiced successfully in Japan. It may also entail revisiting the resources curse argument and the limitations of a commodity-led industrialisation pathway for Africa. This chapter intends to adopt this approach to the industrialisation question for Africa by revisiting some of the historical debates and explanations about Africa's industrialisation in light of new case-study experiences that could serve as new evidence to challenge the conclusions of earlier debates on the subject. The second objective of the chapter is to examine new opportunities and possible new paths for Africa's industrialisation that have been opened up by the changing patterns of global trade. To accomplish both objectives, the chapter will be answering questions like:

i) What lessons do African countries need to draw from the experience of the NICs in light of current structures and patterns of global production?
ii) What would it take for Africa to increase its share in global manufacturing?
iii) What would it take for Africa's products to be involved in more value addition and go up GVCs?
iv) Is a commodity-based industrialisation model still a viable pathway for Africa's industrialisation given its known resources endowment?
v) Is there still a potential role for manufacturing and what other opportunities and alternative pathways for industrialisation remain open for the continent?
vi) What role for regional industrial policy and Africa's practice of developmental regionalism in its industrialisation efforts?

Though the idea is not to answer these questions one after the other, the thrust of the chapter would be to provide reflections in these directions, with the aim of engaging upon discussions that would lead to certain conclusions that would be answering these questions directly. The resultant responses should constitute recommendations for the formulation of domestic and regional industrial policies for the continent's industrialisation within the context of a global drive towards the fourth industrial revolution and its associated opportunities. To accomplish its stated objectives the chapter is divided into six subsections. The section 'Challenges to Industrialisation in Africa' that revisits the challenge to Africa's industrialisation and the reasons why previous industrialisation efforts failed to accomplish their objectives. The section 'Africa's Possibilities to Pursue a Resources-Based Industrialisation Pathway' will explore possible pathways to Africa's industrialisation by examining the debate around commodity-based industrialisation, while the section 'Other Current Industrialisation Possibilities for Africa' examines other new opportunities for Africa's industrialisation offered by the changing patterns of global trade. The section 'Industrialisation within a Developmental Regionalism Paradigm' makes a brief case for Africa's industrialisation within a developmental regionalism paradigm and the final section concludes the chapter.

CHALLENGES TO INDUSTRIALISATION IN AFRICA

The idea that Africa should industrialise is not new. The continent's post-independence leaders – like those in many developing countries in the 1960s and 1970s – looked to state-led, import-substituting industrialisation as the key to rapid economic growth. Though African manufacturing grew in the immediate post-independence period, largely shaped by state-led and protectionist policies, by the mid-1980s, a series of external shocks – including oil price increases, commodity price decreases, real interest rate rises, withering public coffers and the limitations of domestic markets – were major factors in industrial decline in the region (Signe 2018: 3). In addition to these external factors, the industries that were created in these early years were frequently uncompetitive and unsustainable, and efforts to spur industrial development in Africa largely vanished with the economic collapses and structural adjustment programmes (SAPS) of the 1980s and 1990s. The consequences of this first failed episode of industrialisation are that Africa and most African countries have remained largely exporters of unprocessed natural resources with little value addition. This has left them occupying inferior positions in the GVCs of the products which they produce. Despite their manufacturing potential and promising trajectories, most African countries have remained relatively dearth of factories. Africa as a continent has witnessed a systematic decrease in manufacturing's contribution as a percentage of GDP over the last four decades; this at the same time when other regions in the world were experiencing an increase (See Figure 6.1 below).

As illustrated in figure 6.1, the contribution of manufacturing value added as a percentage of GDP has been consistently lower than 18% in Sub-Saharan Africa (SSA) for the last four decades. This confirms both the minimal contribution of manufacturing to GDP and its progressively declining share to below 12% since about the year 2002 and reaching an all-time low in 2010 and 2011. This limited industrial development represents a missed opportunity for economic transformation and quality employment generation that alleviates poverty. This remains a source of concern for the continent given the enormity of the developmental challenges it is facing and remains a continued focus and concern for the continent's policymakers. This remains a policy priority because a robust manufacturing sector is broadly understood as a fundamental path to economic growth and development. The most recent illustration is the launch of the African Continental Free Trade Area (AFCFTA) in March 2018, a single market for goods and services in Africa that aims to unlock manufacturing potential and facilitate industrialisation, driving sustainable growth and jobs among other objectives (Signe 2018: 1). This acknowledgement and sense of urgency from Africa's policymakers is further accentuated by the fact that while Africa was experiencing a decline,

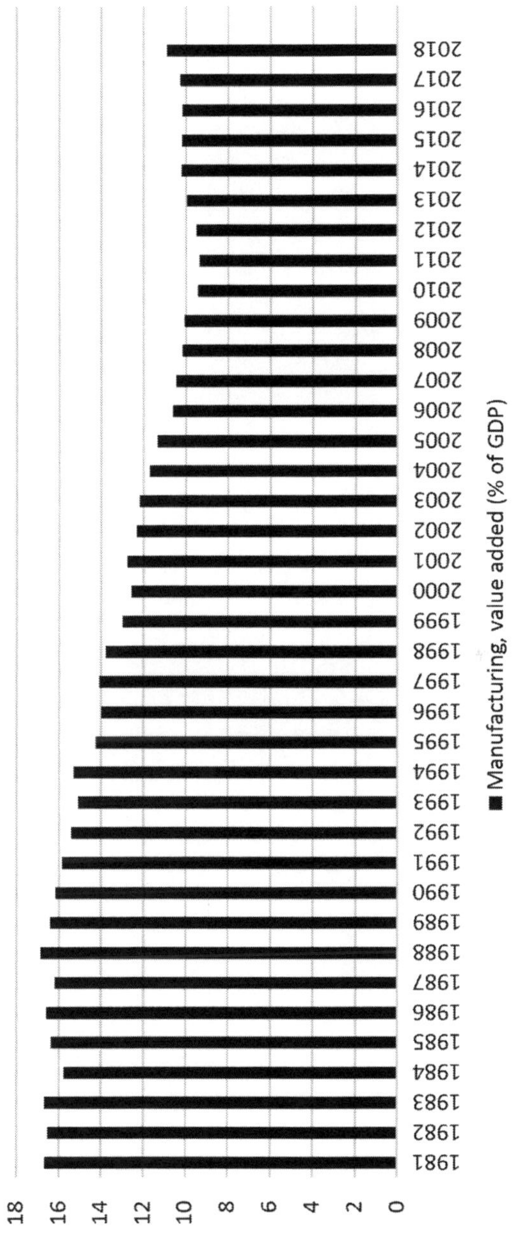

Figure 6.1 Manufacturing, Value Added (% of GDP). *Source*: Author's compilation from World Bank WDI.

other regions in the world were experiencing an increase and a greater contribution of their manufacturing share of GDP. In figure 6.2, the SSA performance is compared with that of East Asia and Pacific, as illustrated below.

As can be seen in figure 6.2, while the manufacturing value added as a percentage of GDP was declining from the mid-2000s in SSA, in the East Asia and Pacific Region the contribution of manufacturing value added as a percentage of GDP was consistently above 20% within that period (2004–2017) and being above 25% between 2004–2008. As an illustration in 2016, Asia alone accounted for about 88% of developing countries gross exports of manufactures to the world, and for 93% of South–South trade in manufactures, while East Asia alone accounted for 72% of both. These trade patterns in Asia have been explained to be the result of a shift from natural resources to manufactured goods.

The main reason the industrialisation gap in Africa with respect to the rest of the world has increased is because of structural weaknesses such as poor infrastructure, weak logistics and trade facilitation, slow regional integration and absence of accreditation frameworks (UNIDO 2016: 13). This is also accompanied by insufficient energy and low information and communications technology which further constrain development. It is estimated that almost 290 million out of 915 million people in SSA have scanty access to electricity. In some African countries, road, rail and freight transport systems date back to colonial times and were focused on moving unprocessed raw materials from extraction zones in the hinterland to coastal areas for onward shipment to international markets (a combination of existing trade and infrastructure development patterns). However, a reliable logistics performance and infrastructure network is critical for trade, economic integration, growth and competitiveness. This includes efficient border management that eliminates shipment delays and enhances predictability in border clearance. In addition to these, there remain coordination challenges among government custom control agencies on regional transit regimes across the continents. There have been efforts aimed at introducing best practices like single windows for trade, automation and risk management also in non-customs control agencies which are all vital for improving trade facilitation. These measures to boost trade facilitation are an important component of industrial competitiveness.

These weaknesses and challenges together partly also explain the low level of merchandise trade amongst African countries, which represented only 11% of total trade between 2007 and 2011 (compared with 50% in Asia and 70% in Europe). Added to this is the failure of African countries to take advantage of lower-than-average labour costs to increase their share of labour-intensive manufacturing. Notwithstanding all these challenges, there is still some optimism about the future of Africa's growth and industrialisation. Some

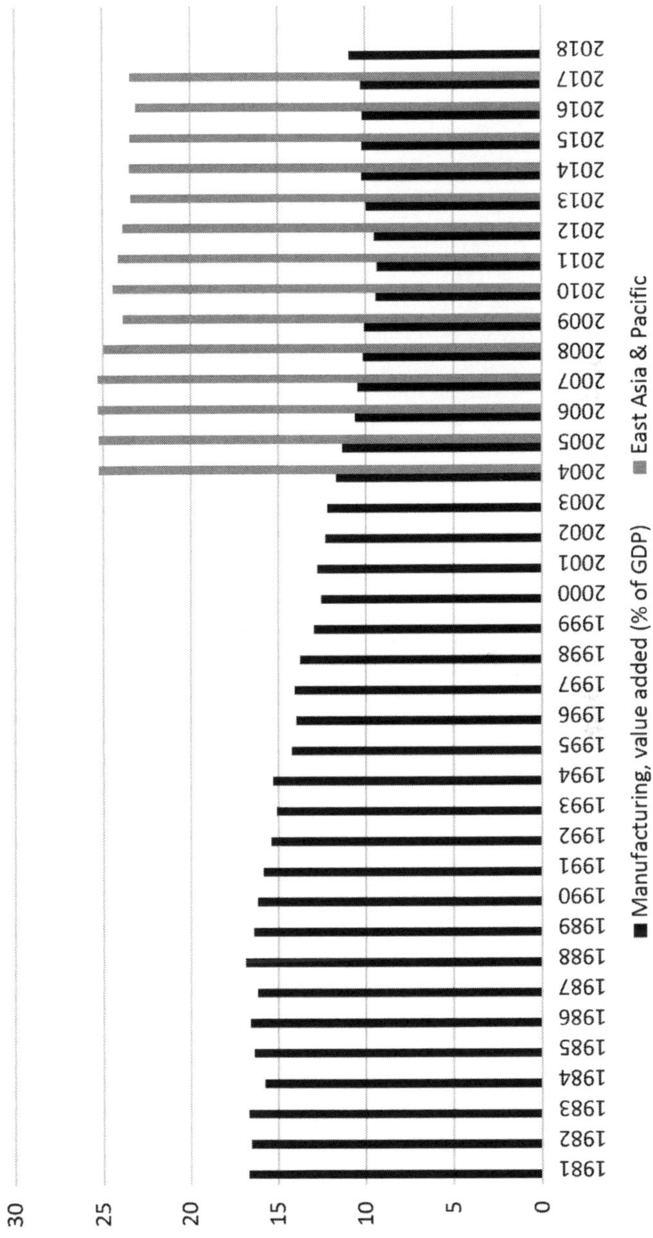

Figure 6.2 Manufacturing, Value Added (% of GDP). *Source*: Author's compilation from World Bank WDI.

authors believe that Africa is likely to be 'the world's next great manufacturing center', potentially capturing part of the 100 million labour-intensive manufacturing jobs that will leave China by 2030. This trend creates a huge opportunity for the continent, not only for countries such as South Africa, Egypt and Nigeria (all regional outperformers in the Global Manufacturing Competitiveness Index) but also for newer players such as Ethiopia, Morocco, Rwanda and others (all of whom have recently adopted policies enabling manufacturing and industrial development) (Signe 2018: 2). This optimism that also accompany the Africa Arising narrative speak to the opportunities that lay ahead of Africa to pursue an industrialisation path taking into account its endowments and contextual realities. For this to happen the continent would have to draw lessons from the industrialisation experience of other regions, as well as the advantages that come with the changing nature of global trade to industrialise. The various options and opportunities that the continent could adopt, drawing lessons from the experience of other regions including its possible industrialisation options shall be examined in the section that follows.

Having clearly articulated the benefits of industrialisation in solving development problems and having clearly highlighted the challenges that limit Africa's industrialisation, this section seeks to explore the opportunities and options open and available for Africa's industrialisation. These opportunities represent a combination of new options that are now open within the context of the fourth industrial revolution as well as contemplation about previously attempted pathways towards industrialisation that could now be more successful due to the lessons that have been learned from past failures and opportunities gathered from the experience of other regions. In this regard, there are opportunities available for Africa's industrialisation through the changing nature of global trade, the unbundling of production and the increased share of global trade in intermediate goods. An analysis of over 400 traded goods in the four traditional GVCs – apparel, footwear, electronics and autos – shows that SSA is not highly integrated into these GVCs, whether via exports or imports. Among these industries, vehicle manufacturing, mainly assembly, often takes the lead in the foreign value added embedded in exports. Other medium-tech manufacturing, such as electrical machinery and metal products, follows a similar structure (UNIDO 2016: 11). In addition to this, the New Industrial Revolution (NIR) – including the Internet of Things, big data, cloud computing, artificial intelligence, robotics, 3D printing, new materials, augmented reality, nanotechnology and biotechnology – has the potential to improve productivity, reduce energy and resource consumption, and thus protect the environment and increase resource efficiency and effectiveness. Though Africa may not currently have the technological endowment to be competitive in this area, it does not preclude it from participating in the opportunities represented by the fourth industrial revolution and the future of production and consumption. Furthermore, there are also opportunities associated with the increased contribution of services in global trade and advantages to be taken of the growing middle-class population on the African continent that represents a potential market for consumer goods. These once treated together with an examination of the natural resources endowment of the continent represent real opportunities for Africa's chosen pathway towards industrialisation. Although each of these components merits extended chapters and even books on their own, they will be treated here in summary forms to highlight some of the key arguments that justify their visitation as both opportunities and suitable pathways for Africa's industrialisation efforts. For ease of presentation, these pathways and opportunities shall be briefly examined in the next two subsections that follow. First through an examination of the opportunities for a resource-based industrialisation pathway in the following section and then through a brief examination of other opportunities for industrialisation that Africa could take advantage as a result of the changing nature of global trade.

AFRICA'S POSSIBILITIES TO PURSUE A RESOURCES-BASED INDUSTRIALISATION PATHWAY

The debate about the possibility of Africa to adopt a resource-based industrialisation pathway is one that is long-standing and ongoing on the continent. The economic logic of this reoccurrence is simple; it seems rational to contemplate an industrialisation pathway for Africa on the basis of its natural resources endowments, seeing that it still has reasonable reserves of a number of globally sought-after natural resources. These become their initial sources of revenue and income upon which they can build to develop industrial and production capacities through value addition and aspirations to climb to higher levels in current GVCs while using the revenues generated during this upgrading to diversify and create industrialisation capacities in other areas. This pathway seems reasonable compared to the no capacity, no possibility of progressive industrialisation, 'resources curse' 'Africa is doomed' narrative that often accompanies discussions about Africa's industrialisation. There is no arguing that in the current context of global trade and the evolution towards the fourth industrial revolution, no single strategy would be necessarily enough but a comprehensive strategy that attempts to develop capacity in a combination of areas, amongst which a focus on its resources. Natural resources have proven to be a blessing in other countries and the recent experience of Asian economies has also proven that comparative advantages and competitive edge are not static deterministic prophecies of people's outcomes but that a combination of right policies and carefully contemplated outcomes can convert the revenue from natural resources to be the source of an economic expansion and deliberate investments in other areas can develop productive capacity that makes countries and regions to become globally competitive and regional production/manufacturing hubs for newly created global markets and changing patterns of global demand.

Seen from this perspective, there are real opportunities to be harnessed for Africa to adopt a natural resources-based pathway to industrialisation as one of the corridors of an industrialisation strategy that has other components as well. This section intends to make a case of why such a strategy is possible for Africa and how it can be achieved. This would have to be part of a comprehensive development strategy that includes an industrial policy that is integrated into a comprehensive strategy to develop national and regional capacities and markets while deliberately working at overcoming the power relations that influence global market access and by proxy GVCs – through a combination of breaking into existing value chains and looking for new opportunities in emerging economies and taking advantage of the emerging global order with the multipolarity of global centres of power and influence.

One must admit that such a transformation for Africa would be coming from a low base and that in many regard the continent is a late starter and latecomer to the space of the control of market access and GVCs, even in the areas of its current resources endowments and once celebrated comparative advantage. African countries are, for example, very lowly placed in the GVCs of some commodities for which they enjoy top-tier positions in global production. For example, Côte d'Ivoire, Ghana, and Nigeria are amongst the world's top exporters of cocoa beans but they individually and collectively own a very tiny percentage of the global market shares for chocolates. In addition, their profiles show remarkably low levels of value addition in their export commodity with only Côte d'Ivoire and Ghana exporting between a fifth and a quarter of their production in semi-processed form, which is in sharp contrast with their Asian and South American counterparts involved in the same industry. Taking the example of some Asian cocoa producers, more than 50% of Indonesia's export value was at the lower and higher end of the semi-processed stages (cocoa paste, butter and powder) and almost all of Malaysia's export value was at the higher end of the semi-processed stage (cocoa butter and powder). In Latin America, Brazil and Mexico have been successful in moving even further up the value chain with one-third of Brazil's and almost all of Mexico's exports consisting of chocolate products (Morris and Fessehaie 2014: 31).

This narrative is important for Africa's commodity-based industrialisation argument because the countries that are cited here (Indonesia, Malaysia,

Mexico, Brazil) were considered to be at comparable levels of development to most African countries in the 1960s. In fact, the ability to significantly increase their value addition in production and even to expand production of agricultural-based export cash crops in Asia and Latin America is what reduced the competitive edge which African commodities had enjoyed in world markets in the period shortly following their independence in the 1960s. They moved from being preferential suppliers of certain commodities to world markets to having to compete with more efficiently produced and consequently cheaper alternatives from Latin America and parts of Asia (the case of palm oil and related products from Malaysia), resulting in a decrease in their global share of trade even in unprocessed primary commodities in world markets. So although there are political economy issues with tariff and non-tariff technical barriers to market access in the advanced economies of the North (high tariffs and taxes placed upon some processed goods than on raw unprocessed commodities) which cause the rents to be disproportionately located in these northern economies (Swiss chocolate factories and European fortress protection of its agricultural sector), African economies cannot resort to victimhood because as indicated in the above passages, some countries in Latin America and Asia have been able to overcome these barriers to global market access, value addition in production and progress along GVCs, and all Africa needs to do is to emulate the examples of these countries.

One of the ways in which African countries can successfully pursue a natural resources-based industrialisation pathway is through the promotion of forward and backward linkages in the areas of their current resource endowments and production. For African countries endowed with natural resources, the recent developments in commodity markets present an added opportunity to promote industrialisation and knowledge intensification processes around backward and forward linkages to the commodity sectors. Morris and Fessehaie (2014: 29) referencing an Albert Hirschman (1981) framework identify three possible linkages that African countries could adopt to pursue a commodity-based industrialisation pathway. These are possible *fiscal linkages, consumption linkages* and *production linkages*. With respect to fiscal linkages, they argue that the resource rents which the government is able to harvest from the commodity sectors in the form of corporate taxes, royalties and income taxes can be used to promote industrial development in sectors unrelated to commodities.

There is a lot that Africa needs to learn in this regard from other resource-rich countries like the Nordic countries and the countries in the Middle East. There is, for example, The Abu Dhabi Investment Authority (ADIA), a Sovereign Wealth Fund (SWF) owned by the Emirate of Abu Dhabi (in the United Arab Emirates) and founded for the purpose of investing funds on behalf of the Government of the Emirate of Abu Dhabi. It manages the

Emirate's excess oil reserves, estimated to be as much as $875 billion. In the Nordic Countries, Norway also established a SWF to manage the proceeds of its oil revenue derived from the North Sea Oil fields called The Government Pension Fund of Norway. It comprises of two entirely separate SWFs owned by the government of Norway. The Government Pension Fund Global, also known as the Oil Fund, was established in 1990 to invest the surplus revenues of the Norwegian petroleum sector. It has over US $1 trillion in assets, including 1.4% of global stocks and shares, making it one of the world's largest SWF. (In May 2018 it was worth about $195,000 per Norwegian citizen).

There are many examples of this nature that exists and could strengthen the thesis of the fiscal linkage for the ownership of resources for African countries that could become an important financing source for Africa's industrialisation. This example dispels the traditional 'resources curse' argument as concerns the usage of Africa's resources and makes the argument that it is not the presence of natural resources that predisposes a country to a certain 'cursed' series of outcomes but the usage of those resources. As far as this is related to the industrialisation debate, it makes the case in favour of commodity-based industrialisation because it could constitute the basis for important learning through the development of technological capacity while also being an important source of financing for industrialisation capacity in order sectors. This is, for example, how the Emirates used their oil wealth to develop Dubai into an attractive touristic destination and business hub with a booming real estate market and increasing capacities in the financial services industries while becoming a trading hub for the region. These have been supplemented with a number of globally competitive airlines that make these countries an effective transition hub for travellers coming from all over the world. It took visionary leadership and the decision to intentionally invest the initial oil wealth in specific avenues to develop other sectors of the economy, which is the nexus of the fiscal linkage argument.

The other two forms of linkages that Africa's commodity-based industrialisation could explore and be based upon are the consumption linkages and production linkages. With regards to consumption linkages, this relates to the demand for the output of other sectors arising from the incomes earned in the commodity sector has the potential to provide a major spur to industrial production as all incomes (whether salaries, wages or profits) earned in the resource sector are spent on products and services. This has to do with the coordinated stimulus that will be released upon the economy through spurring expenditure as a result of the incomes earned from the commodity-based industrialisation process. This has the effect of direct demand stimuli for consumer goods and the spillover effects of the consumption of a rising middle class. This linkage is closely tied to the production linkages.

This relates to both the forward (processing commodities) and backward (producing inputs to be utilised in commodity production) linkages of the industrialisation process.

Hirschman (1981) argues in this regard that production linkages pave a path for industrial diversification. This, for example, would relate to the development of a *petrochemical industry* (and the learning associated with it thereof) that comes as a result of the ownership and exploration of oil deposits. The petrochemical industry is an industry branch that produces organic intermediate products such as refinery products, natural gas, plastic, rubber, fibre raw materials. This industry is competitive, involves significant technological innovation, is capital-intensive and operates in a global product market. In terms of production volumes, the industry represents approximately 10% of the total petroleum industry. Historically, the industry evolved out of technological innovation in the developed industrialised economies. Until the last quarter of the twentieth century, the production of petrochemicals was concentrated in Western Europe, the United States and Japan. Over the last few decades, however, production in areas with competitively priced feedstocks has increased dramatically. New production capacity has been built in the Middle East and Asia. This new capacity employs the latest technologies on the largest scales with some of the cheapest available feedstocks and, as a result, has changed the competitive landscape of the industry. Many older facilities using higher-cost feedstocks have not been able to compete and hence there have been site closures, especially in the more established and mature European markets (Clews 2016).

This brief narrative about the petrochemical industry holds two fundamental truths for Africa's industrialisation. The first is *that competitive advantages are not static and indefinitely skewed in favour of certain economies, and if countries invest in developing their competitive edge in any domain, they can overtake those who have traditionally been presented as the owners of the competitive advantage.* The second lesson for Africa's industrialisation is the fact that *there are opportunities for diversification beyond the current stock of natural resources.* The desire to move up GVCs of existing resources that African countries own ought to be an express priority and objective for their host economies, as well as the exploration of possibilities for industrial diversification based on the current endowment of resources. These must never be treated as quick-fix solutions but as part of long-term plans to develop the capacity to move up existing production value chains, create alternative industries, access current markets and take advantage of the demographic dividend on the African continent to anticipate the creation of newer markets that would justify industrialisation at a certain scale. This ought to be the real focus of African solidarity as opposed to a simple focus and emphasis on market integration.

Though there is this emphasis on the opportunities that come with resources-based industrialisation for Africa, resource-based industrialisation strategies are subject to three main types of criticism:

i) *resource-based industrialisation is as difficult as any other industrialisation path;*
ii) *commodity sectors are not likely to promote linkages and externalities: and*
iii) *resource-based industries do not match Africa's factor endowments (Morris and Fessehaie 2014: 29).*

The first criticism is a reality check regarding the fact that the ownership of resources is not a guarantee that industrialisation and diversification will automatically take place. Wherever these have been found to occur, they are often the result of deliberate policies to produce the same. As much as the argument has been made that ownership of resources is not a curse, it is important to equally argue that resources ownership must be accompanied by requisite capacity-building measures to take full advantage of the benefits of resources ownership, as countries like Norway have done and seen the development of an elaborate petrochemical industry alongside the mere exploration and sale of oil reserves to generate revenue. This brings to the fore the importance of factors such as *infrastructure, human capital, access to financial capital, technology and skills* which are all important in determining the benefits that may accrue to any country from the ownership of natural resources. The usage of the revenue from the exploration of owned resources through the three aforementioned linkages through deliberate policy interventions and action is what ultimately determines a country's competitiveness, position and growth along the GVC of its selected product. As Morris and Fessehaie (2014) argue, the experience of resource-rich Venezuela, Argentina, Malaysia and Thailand suggests that the export success of resource-based industries was not so much the result of high level of initial skills and capital, but rather *economic policies fostering their accumulation.* Though the experiences of these countries may vary greatly, the lessons from the more successful ones amongst them point to the fact that it will require deliberate policy action to make the best of the ownership of natural resources for the adoption of a natural resources-based industrialisation pathway and to utilise the resources-generated rents to create broader-based and more dynamic growth trajectories (diversifying into services industries, for example).

This suggests that there is hope for Africa through the pursuit of a resources-based industrialisation pathway. The experience of other countries offers hope in the fact that Africa indeed stands a chance to make a difference with the use of its resources, if it can learn and implement the lessons that other countries have to offer in their own industrialisation efforts from a resources base. For example, *commodity sectors have promoted technologically sophisticated upstream industries in 'new' resource-rich countries (Australia, Norway, Scotland).* With the right policies and under the right conditions, commodity production can have a positive impact on technological deepening, manufacturing and service upstream/downstream activities, and ultimately growth (Morris and Fessehaie 2014: 29). In addition to this, the historical experience of many resource-rich countries shows that commodity sectors foster productivity growth, technological innovation, forward and backward linkages, provided they are supported by good institutions and investment in human capital and knowledge (de Ferranti et al. 2002). If this has been the case in other countries and regions, there is no reason why it would not be the same in Africa. The question should therefore not be whether Africa can industrialise based on its natural resources endowment but rather how this can be achieved through the promotion of linkage development, value addition and the diversification into new avenues making use of the rents accumulated from the resources sector to invest into the development of capability in other areas and sectors like the development of technological capabilities in related and associated industries and diversification into other aspects of the production value chain. There are ample opportunities and examples for Africa to delve into alternative and related paths of industrialisation and participating in GVC and some of these options are briefly examined in the subsection that follows.

OTHER CURRENT INDUSTRIALISATION POSSIBILITIES FOR AFRICA

There are opportunities for Africa's industrialisation presented by the changing patterns of global trade because global trade flows have been increasingly characterised by intra-industry trade in intermediate goods. This reflects trade between lead firms and their suppliers around the world. It represents an opportunity for Africa's industrialisation because, unlike the days of import-substitution industrialisation in Africa, there is an opportunity not only to produce complete finished products to be sent to the global market which may require more varied sets of skills and capabilities, but there could be the production of intermediate products based on Africa's natural resource endowments that feed into. Now, whilst Africa's degree of export orientation and import penetration is high, imports are largely composed of final consumer goods and exports of raw materials. Imports of capital equipment and many intermediaries are primarily destined for commodity extraction. This can however be quickly changed by two important factors that characterise the continent, the demographic dividend of a rising middle class that could constitute an effective labour force and a consumer market for finished goods and the potential for the creation of larger markets that could come with furthering regional integration, including the expected gains of the just concluded AFCFTA. In this regard, a 2016 UNIDO report to the G20 Development Working Group (DWG) noted that the fragmentation of the African market is very costly for all African countries. The report recommended that industrial agglomerations and other growth benefits could be realised from the development of transport, logistics and industrial corridors and hub development around transport nodes and important urban centres. These together represent the formulation of industrial policies not just based upon existing markets but the deliberate commitment to create larger markets through furthering economic integration by uplifting the trade and non-trade related barriers to trade. This is perhaps why preferential liberalisation of service trade now features in many regional trading arrangements, and the LDC service waiver of the World Trade Organization (WTO) opens the possibility of making them more widely available on a non-reciprocal basis.

So there are indeed encouraging patterns of global trade that represent real opportunities for Africa's continued quest for industrialisation through the creation of opportunities to be integrated into GVCs. GVCs refer to the different value-added links, composed of many activities, required to bring a product from conception and design to its delivery to the final consumer and, finally, to its disposal (Kaplinsky and Morris 2001). GVCs are composed of various stages characterised by varying levels of value addition and, crucially, by different entry barriers. Higher entry barriers are usually created by skills, R&D and technology. It is these barriers that allow countries and firms to capture high rents, because there are fewer competitors and such rents are also high in activities associated with design, marketing and distribution (Morris and Fessehaie 2014: 26). All Africa needs to do in this regard is to overcome these entry barriers through a deliberate accumulation of skills and technology that builds both capacity and competency in specific selected industries. Like every process of R&D investment, skills accumulation, innovation and technology acquisition, this will require long-term deliberate and strategic investments that may yield their fruits only over time. This could be done both with the intention of tapping into existing markets and GVCs in the short run while making preparations to supply the needs of future markets and consumer demand. There is no saying that there is path dependency as to the pathway and trajectory of development that African economies need to follow but there are real opportunities to be harnessed from the economic transformation that comes with industrialisation that is accompanied by the readiness to provide new consumer goods for the products that its expanding population would need. Without advocating for an autarkic philosophy of anticipated production, it is both prudential macroeconomic management (from a balance of trade and balance of payment perspective) for Africa to anticipate well ahead of time being able to produce a significant proportion of the consumption needs of its current and future population and integrate market as shall be adapted to their tastes and preferences as they evolve.

Some authors have argued in this regard that breaking into global markets for manufacturing, agro-industry and tradable services represents Africa's only viable path to accelerated structural change and industrialisation. Such industries can be served by micro, small and medium-sized enterprises, using their relative advantages in flexibility, innovativeness, personalised contacts, quality of products and creating new opportunities for the international sourcing of scarce specialised skills. This gives considerable scope for the African private sector to become a part of the industrialisation process in partnership with their governments and regional organisations who shall provide them the support and policy environment to contribute their innovativeness in such industrialisation efforts. This option makes a lot of sense for Africa because current trends in intermediate goods trade are indicative of regional and GVC integration, as fragmented production processes require parts, components and partially manufactured sub-assemblies to cross borders, sometimes more than once, before goods are produced and shipped to consumer markets. At the moment, Africa is only capturing a small but growing share of this global trade in intermediaries, which rose from 1.4% in 1995 to 2.2% in 2011. Almost three-quarters of this growth was due to backward integration (the share of foreign value added embedded in a country's exports) (UNIDO 2016: 11). For Africa to increase its share in this global trade in intermediary goods and effectively leverage the possibilities that lay in its regional industrialisation efforts, it would urgently need to close the knowledge gap with industry in other regions. This again highlights the role of knowledge in production – both in terms of the role of technology and that of firm capabilities. Upgrading national and regional production capabilities should be integrated into national and regional industrial policies and become as much a point of emphasis as have been market access and expansion through further integration.

The potential to do this at the regional and continental scale is huge and this remains the core of the developmental regionalism argument. Industrial development opens up opportunities for positive externalities that are difficult to quantify. Through cooperation at the regional and continental levels, African countries can promote diversification of technological capabilities and their skills base by developing backward linkage supply firms to the commodity sectors and resource-processing industries. The variety of technological capabilities and skills fostered in linkages also opens up opportunities for lateral migration into other sectors. This can be pursued anchoring upon the experience of slightly more advanced industrial hubs in various sub regions to promote the flying geese model of industrialisation as Japan was for its surrounding Asian neighbours.

The flying geese model explains the shifting competitiveness of an industry over time by focussing on the dynamic changes in factor endowments (labour and capital) that countries usually experience during economic development. FDIs, besides triggering an indigenous improvement in the availability and quality of factor endowments in the countries catching up from behind, also help promote the transformation of trade structures by transferring factors of production (capital, technology and management know-how) from the more advanced countries to the less developed ones (Hiley 2000: 62). This could be the approach/model adopted in African countries to pursue industrialisation around anchor countries and sub-regional industrial hubs, like South Africa in the Southern Africa or Kenya and Tanzania in East Africa. The dynamics could be different for West Africa and Northern Africa, but the principle could more or less be the same, emphasising on the leadership of a regional leader. The industrial policies and development of these regional leaders could also serve as an anchor of the industrialisation strategy of the rest of the region, with its progression along the manufacturing line leading it to give way to other countries while it progresses to the production of more advanced goods. This can create a mutually beneficial and symbiotic relationship amongst countries participating in a regional integration arrangement even if they are at different levels of production and technological intensity in their manufacturing capacity, for example.

Drawing some inspiration from the case of Asia, the NICs started to accept FDI from Japan, Europe and the United States before other regions did so. Consequently, at the beginning of the 1970s, they suddenly emerged as international export bases in the global economy. The FDI route to join the global economy was different from the path which Japan had followed. Japan achieved growth through import substitution using technology introduced from abroad. In the same token, the development of South Korea's industry was initially never expanded beyond textiles and home electric appliances because the range of Japanese FDI was limited to these industries (Hiley 2000: 63). Africa can follow in these footsteps because there is considerable scope for African countries at different levels of industrialisation to benefit mutually from the flying geese pattern of trade and FDI. As long as they pursue appropriate industrial and technology policies geared towards the export market, these countries can move up the industrial hierarchy through accelerated capital accumulation and the adaptation of advanced technology in such a way that shifts competitiveness to the mutual advantage of all countries and does not lead to unmanageable dislocations and adjustment problems or trade frictions (Hiley 2000: 65).

This could be applied in Southern Africa, for example, in the minerals sector, for which the ownership and exploration of minerals and natural resources is a common characteristic amongst some countries (Angola, Mozambique, Botswana, Namibia, Zambia, Zimbabwe and South Africa, for example). The resources endowments of these countries in the minerals and natural resources sector (oil and gas in the case of Angola, Mozambique and recently South Africa) constitute a comparative advantage which could facilitate the formation of a new regionally oriented, minerals-based industrialisation strategy. As these economies develop, and as a response to the changing economic environment, there is no reason why these Southern African economies should not undergo significant structural change and readjustment in the future. They could aim to maintain their comparative advantage in the minerals sector whilst developing and moving into labour-intensive and human capital-intensive manufactures before finally developing a comparative advantage in technology-intensive manufactures, passing the outdated industries down the ladder in line with the flying geese pattern of economic development (Hiley 2000: 70). This calls for a different approach to the formulation of national industrial policy that is coordinated along with regional industrial policies. Its successful application at the level of Southern Africa implies that it can be replicated at the continental level. Industrialisation is thus possible within the developmental regionalism paradigm, but it imposes a unique responsibility upon national and regional organisations in the development of their industrialisation policy and strategy. The extent to which national and regional policies could be utilised for the advancement of an industrialisation agenda within a developmental regionalism paradigm is the subject of the next section.

INDUSTRIALISATION WITHIN A DEVELOPMENTAL REGIONALISM PARADIGM

In the pursuit of industrialisation within a developmental regionalism paradigm in Africa, there are various roles to be played by national and regional industrialisation policies. These roles are closely linked to the responsibility of national governments and regional/continental organisations who together share the responsibility for the formulation and implementation of policies that would effectively lead to economic transformation and the industrialisation of the continent. These policies would have to be enacted and implemented at the national level and mainstreamed for adoption and implementation at the regional level through effective coordination and strategic cooperation. It takes growing and industrialising countries to make for growing and industrialising regions and the continent. The impetus would not only come from the sub-regional organisations if the drive is not nurtured at the level of the country. In the same token, individual country efforts could be limited in scope and reach if they fail to take advantage of opportunities that can be created by sub-regional and continental integration. Seen from this perspective, the question of Africa's industrialisation then becomes one of determining what the national authorities ought to be doing and what regional authorities ought to be doing in return and how their combined efforts ought to be coordinated to drive the industrialisation agenda in a true developmental regionalism approach.

The East Asian experience has shown in this regard that what worked best for national economies were macroeconomic and structural policies that enabled the private sector to play a leading role in the growth process; policies to boost domestic savings and FDI; effective use of foreign aid and sound external debt management. Their experience further demonstrates what can be achieved with a combination of pragmatic and sensible government policies and a disciplined and hardworking population that responds to the right incentives (Hiley 2000: 59). Therefore to emulate their example, African countries would need to promote an active role for the state in promoting industrial development (through the adoption of pragmatic as opposed to ideologically driven policy positions and the development and training of a disciplined and hardworking labour force) working together or in sync with the private sector. To adopt a pragmatic approach and move away from ideological pockets of market fundamentalism, Africa would need to move away from the debate of whether or not the state should be involved in the promotion of industrialisation to settle on defining the role the state ought to play in promoting industrialisation and structural change. In the same token, there seems to also be a consensus that public action needs to move beyond the regulatory reform agenda pushed by the international financial institutions to address the physical, institutional and knowledge constraints limiting Africa's industrial development (Ajakaiye and Page 2012: ii6). Reforms are important but insufficient conditions to promote a certain kind and intensity of industrial production, especially where production capacity is low and technology scanty. These amongst other considerations ought to constitute a more comprehensive agenda for policymakers involved in and interested in the promotion of industrialisation. The components of this agenda ought to include but are not limited to the following:

i) Infrastructure and new skills are central to any attempt to create globally competitive industry.

ii) Spatial industrial policies in the form of well-functioning special economic zones (SEZs) have been poorly implemented in the region and offer considerable promise.
iii) FDI is a key tool to acquire knowledge and needs to be effectively promoted.
iv) Fiscal incentives should be time-bound, reward first movers and subject to rigorous evaluation.

When these elements are embedded in national industrial policies, they should equally become the connecting points into regional industrial policy frameworks. Through a synchronisation of national and regional industrial policy, industrialisation would be able to be achieved within a developmental regionalism framework. The developmental regionalism framework advocates for conscious and planned policy actions aimed at building the productive capacities of member countries and promoting industrial restructuring. As argued in the previous chapter, the agenda has to extend beyond tariffs and non-tariff measures, import and export quotas and bans, technical and phytosanitary standards, to include issues such as *competition policy*, *the provision of infrastructure and other public goods*, *investment*, *promotion of research and development and building the domestic productive capacities* of *both the private sector and state-owned enterprises* to ensure the greatest impact and efficiency. Within this framework, the emphasis of developmental regionalism is on facilitating industrial restructuring and economic transformation through coordination efforts at the regional and continental level for the implementation of 'strategic' *trade policies* that are *consistent with the domestic industrial policy frameworks* of the states involved.

Going beyond a mere emphasis on market integration, developmental regionalism promotes 'gradual and sequenced trade liberalization' that is combined with policy actions, such as *coordinated investments into regional transport infrastructure*, in order to *improve linkages between the states involved* and *enhance the productive capacities of the region (sub-regional emphasis that builds into continent-wide capacity)*. Developmental regionalism therefore also thrives through the promotion of policy harmonisation among participating countries in a regional arrangement and its promotion goes hand in hand with the strengthening of the *structures, institutions and capabilities* of national governments to implement such policies (UNCTAD 2013: 97).

As argued in the previous chapter, the four key 'policy tools and drivers' for fostering developmental regionalism in Africa are *industrial policy*, *the use of development corridors that improve trade-related infrastructure, the establishment of SEZs and the promotion of regional value chains*. In pursuing these four avenues as a collective, it is expected that developmental regionalism would facilitate industrial restructuring and economic transformation through the implementation of 'strategic' trade policies that are consistent with the domestic industrial policy frameworks of the states involved. Developmental regionalism for industrialisation goes beyond superficial commitments to market integration that are heavily constrained by other obstacles. It is a joint pursuit of the development of productive capacity, the creation of expanded markets and the coordination of national and regional industrial policies. Through the establishment of regional development corridors and SEZs, the promotion of regional value chains and investment in business facilitation infrastructure, education and capacity development initiatives at sub-regional and continental levels, the industrialisation of the continent becomes a possibility within a developmental regionalism framework.

CONCLUSION

This chapter has examined the possible pathways that Africa could adopt in the pursuit of its industrialisation. It has adopted an approach that is in line with the thinking that is not focusing on answering the question of whether industrialisation is an option for Africa, but builds from the understanding or assumption that it is a necessity. It has made the case that there are many lessons to be learnt from Africa's past industrialisation efforts that could inform its current and future quest towards industrialisation. It has in this regard revisited the debate about the resource curse and made the argument that natural resources were not a hindrance in other regions of the world but constituted the basis for industrialisation through the creation of linkages, then Africa's resources can be used as a basis or take-off point for its industrialisation. It has also made the argument that there are also new opportunities available to Africa represented by the changing nature of global trade that could make it possible for Africa's industrialisation to adopt paths today that were perhaps not possible in the past. With a population dividend and an emerging middle class, coupled with an increase in the quality of its human capital endowment through education and deliberate skills acquisition, and the implementation of a well-crafted industrial policy coordinated at the national and regional level, there should be considerable scope to make progress in the advancement of Africa's industrialisation agenda. Such a coordinated approach will help the rapidly growing African economies to answer the central question they have been facing recently, that of how to use the dividends of their recent economic growth to foster industrialisation and thereby facilitate general development. There is also sufficient scope for such initiatives to be pursued at the national, sub-regional and continental levels as ought to be the case within a developmental regionalism paradigm.

To get to that level Africa would have to deal with the scale and scope of the under-provision of regional public goods, particularly infrastructure, as well as coordinated knowledge generation and harmonised trade and investment regimes among countries (UNIDO 2016: 14). This can be accomplished through the inclusion of these priorities in national and sub-regional industrial policies, whose adoption and implementation would become part of the continental industrialisation effort.

As part of this continent-wide industrialisation effort, cross-border infrastructure has to be made widely accessible and reliable, supported by institutional harmonisation in the trade regime, to increase productivity and competitiveness. It is also worth saying that given the diversity of resource endowment, differences in stages of development and economic background between the different geographical regions of Africa, there can be no 'one size fits all' industrialisation strategy. There are however certain approaches to the accumulation of industrial capabilities and focal sectors that could be a common and shared experience all across the continent. African countries could, for example, focus on strategies for the development of a modern service economy (tourism, IT, transport) and low- and medium-technology manufacturing development as a point of departure while aiming to create and serve large domestic and regional markets. There should also be opportunities for the development of resource-based industrialisation in countries rich in natural resources. Indeed, each country and region on the continent is likely to have a multifaceted approach to industrialisation and pursue more than one strategy (Morris and Fessehaie 2014: 29).

These strategies would have to be accompanied by some consistency between trade and industrial strategies as pivotal elements to foster regional integration, within a developmental regionalism paradigm. In this regard, African countries and their regional organisations will have to move away from 'generalized' industrial policies that have proven ineffective over the last three decades. They will also need to still build strong institutions and viable investment climates and to prioritise and explore the full potential of public–private partnerships (PPPs) and the opportunities for collaboration among industry, governments and other stakeholders. With these, they would be able to make use of the advantages that come with resources ownership to develop a well-coordinated resources-based industrialisation strategy and pathway, while taking advantage of the new and emerging opportunities that are represented by the changing patterns of global trade.

Chapter 7

The Future of African Integration, Emerging Issues and the Implications for the Developmental Regionalism Paradigm

INTRODUCTION

As we wrap up the final chapter of this manuscript, the world is in a place of turmoil in the middle of 2022. It has been barely a couple of months since the reopening of the world economy to global travel and tourism following the coronavirus (COVID-19) global pandemic. As some travel restrictions were being lifted and the global economy began to recover from the pandemic, war broke out between Russia and Ukraine that has had serious implications on global fuel prices in almost every economy and is causing serious shortages in some economies that received their supply of wheat and grain from Ukraine. In a March 2022 article on the global economic impacts of the Russia–Ukraine war, the *Economist* magazine argues that the conflict between Russia and Ukraine will affect the global economy via three main channels: financial sanctions, commodities prices and supply-chain disruptions. The paper goes on to argue that the most serious effect of the Russia–Ukraine conflict on the world economy will come in the form of higher commodities prices. Commodities prices could jump owing to three factors: concerns around supplies, the destruction of physical infrastructure and sanctions. The global impact of this conflict on commodity prices in particular is due to the fact that taken together, Ukraine and Russia account for more than a quarter of the global wheat trade and produce 12% of calories consumed globally.

According to the Bloomberg Africa desk, the African Development Bank is responding to this reality by mobilising funds to increase wheat production in Africa. This is being done through a $1 billion plan to boost wheat production in Africa in order to avert what they called 'potential food shortages arising from Russia's invasion of Ukraine'. So the African Development Bank is raising the funds to help 40 million African farmers utilise climate-resilient technologies and increase their output of heat-tolerant wheat varieties and other crops.

According to Human Rights Watch, countries in East, West, Middle and Southern Africa, including Angola, Cameroon, Kenya and Nigeria, were already grappling with soaring food prices due to extreme climate and weather events such as floods, landslides and droughts, and the COVID-19 pandemic, which disrupted production efforts and global supply chains. Russia and Ukraine are among the top five global exporters of barley, sunflower and maize, and account for about a third of the world's wheat exports. Nigeria, the world's fourth largest wheat importer, receives a fourth of its imports from Russia and Ukraine. Cameroon, Tanzania, Uganda and Sudan source more than 40% of their wheat imports from Russia and Ukraine. However, the combined population of Ukraine (at about 37 million) from whom Nigeria is dependent for a significant percentage of its food inputs is less than 20% of the population of Nigeria.

Far from being interested in commenting on the merits of the Russia–Ukraine conflict, at the risk of starting off on a new subject while closing this volume, the purpose of starting this concluding chapter with this contemporary global challenge has been to highlight the continued vulnerability that characterises the African reality. In the same token, as has been the message hopefully throughout this volume, the possibilities and opportunities that lay before the continent if it would recognise these opportunities and convert them for its benefits. For example, disruptions in the supply of wheat and other exports from Russia and Ukraine could represent an opportunity for African countries to develop the capacity to replace these products in their domestic food baskets and even push the frontiers to become global producers as well and why not take up some of the market shares that may have been created as a result of reduced production from the countries in conflict.

This book has been about a message of hope for the African continent to arise and take its place within the global community of nations, by addressing the challenges that it has customarily faced (like conflicts, poverty and food insecurity) by turning the page of its past and history, doing a few things differently, taking advantage of the recent economic booms and the continued discovery of resources around the continent to develop the abilities to become a respectable and significant global player. In this regard it has been argued thus far that with the advantage of growing economies, a demographic dividend with a rising middle class, rising levels of education and literacy across the continent, reduced levels of conflicts and increased inflows of investments to the continent, Africa now has the possibility of reinventing itself, changing the narrative of its past of underdevelopment and positioning itself to be a key global player in the future, if only it succeeds to learn the appropriate lessons from its own experience and the experience of other regions who have succeeded to uplift their people out of poverty and position themselves to be prosperous middle-income or emerging economies. It is of course important to mention at this point that the upliftment being discussed in this manner has to do with the shared prosperity of some 54 nations that admittedly have different political systems, economic endowments, capacities, institutions, geographical limitations and a range of challenges that stand in the way of development. It goes without saying that these countries would have to individually enjoy prosperity for the region to be uplifted but more specifically they would have to learn to put in place mechanisms of shared prosperity. Talking of mechanisms of shared prosperity, the much-taunted Japanese flying geese model comes to mind, where a rising economy undergoing industrial transformation lifts other surrounding economies along with itself to result in a prosperous region. This was a scenario in the context of industrialisation, the unbundling of manufacturing production, growth in technology intensity that saw lower-tech component parts being transferred to neighbouring countries, while the leading nation advanced in innovation and higher-end production technologies and together they formed a vibrant market through regional integration deepening and broadening the contribution to the shared prosperity narrative of the so-called Asian Tigers.

Is Africa capable of replicating such a shared model of prosperity and collectivisation of benefits and action for its development is a question that remains to be answered. Can development be pursued as a collective initiative and objective in a more deliberate manner outside of regional integration or market integration objectives or is it the natural outcome of regional integration through the creation of larger markets that have been argued within the literature to be beneficial? Is development a by-product of regional integration or should its attainment be the object of deliberate policy initiatives towards its promotion as part of the integration arrangements, would regional integration be conducted differently were it to take on an intentional developmental mandate? If yes, what would be the principal components of the differences and if no why not. In the specific case of Africa, should the development objective be left to the benevolence of the integration process or should the pursuit of development through integration become the preferred approach towards Africa's development, what would a development-centred approach to integration looks like and how different would it be from the current approach and practice of integration. These and questions of this nature are some of the fundamental challenges that need to be resolved within the discourse on Africa's approach to collective development through the pursuit of regional integration.

Thus far, this volume has made the argument that indeed it is possible to pursue collective development and still attain the objectives of regional integration through the adoption of a developmental regionalism paradigm. It has been argued that this 'development integration' approach (developmental regionalism) entails the adoption of both macro and micro coordination in a multisectoral program embracing production, infrastructure and trade, as well as ensuring a more equitable balance from the benefits of regional integration by complementing efforts towards trade integration by efforts *towards regional industrial development*. Defining developmental regionalism in this instance as cooperation among countries in a broader range of areas that could include investment, research and development, as well as policies aimed at accelerating regional industrial development and regional infrastructure provision, such as building up better networks of roads and railway (UNCTAD 2013).

THE FUTURE OF AFRICA'S DEVELOPMENT, NEW OPPORTUNITIES, AND THE DEVELOPMENTAL REGIONALISM QUESTION

There are quite a few recent developments on the continent and beyond that spell hope for its joint pursuit of regional integration and development. There are new players in the development space that bring new dynamics and opportunities for Africa's development, increasing competition and the potential benefits of a variety of development partners on the table. There is the often spoken-off impact of the BRICS alliance and the opportunities it could offer Africa, including much talks about expanding its membership to other African countries. Along with this is the frequently discussed role of China and its approach to partnership and collaboration with African countries that could represent both an opportunity and a threat Africa would have to learn to take better advantage of the potential opportunities while mitigating the threats that may seek to roll back some of its accumulated gains from over the years. The 'China effect' and certainly the role of new partners moving into the continent, together with the changing role of traditional development partners in Africa are worthy of an exclusive analysis that goes beyond the scope of this volume. Across economic, political and security domains, the growth of China's presence in Africa has been swift and staggering, which has fed both simplistic caricatures of China's role on the continent and fears of renewed geopolitical competition. However, Lloyd Thrall (2015), in a report from the RAND Corporation on China's expanding African relations, argues that a closer look at China's involvement on the continent would reveal a more balanced picture. Their report argues that a range of stakeholders and interests drive China's engagement on the continent, including the following:

- China's government and commercial actors have three primary economic interests in Africa: a source for natural resource imports, a growing

and relatively underutilised market for exports and investment and an opportunity for Chinese firms to increase employment and gain global experience.
- China's principal political interests in Africa include bolstering China's international image and influence, isolating Taiwan, countering problematic international norms and supporting the stability of economic partners.
- China's emerging security interests in Africa are driven by Beijing's larger interests in safeguarding economic development and increasing political influence. Its foremost emerging security interest is protecting the growing number of citizens and assets from internal instability, popular backlash, terrorism and kidnapping.

From infrastructural development to concessional loans, China's contribution to Africa's development can hardly be considered negligible although the question of whether or not its presence has been beneficial to the continent remains debatable. What however remains important in our sense is that Africa and Africans would have to engage with China (as with all its partners for that matter) in a manner that pursues and entrenches its own strategic interests first and then seeks to arrive at outcomes that are mutually beneficial to it and its partners. This seems to be the approach adopted by other countries and regions of the world and there is no reason why this should not be the case for Africa.

This also has to be seen within the debate on the multipolarity of the global economy and Africa's place in this changing future of global dynamics. Africa needs to position itself increasingly as a player in that configuration as opposed to a passive recipient of the strategic actions of global actors. It has the demographic dividend and geopolitical location to become an important actor and as has been the argument of this volume, getting its integration right and deriving the resultant benefits can prove to be quite key to that process. This debate of the implication for Africa's development on the multipolarity of the world, and/or the declining influence (if at all) of the Western hegemony with the rise of Eastern Giants, interpreted together with the consequent changes in the policies and approaches of traditional partners could represent some real opportunities for Africa, Africa's development and the adoption of the developmental regionalism paradigm. Without going into the details of these debates at this point, it may be sufficient to say that it is very important if not imperative for African countries and the continental coordination mechanisms to prepare to take advantage of whatever opportunities these changes come with, as well as position the continent to be part of the drivers of these global changes while articulating their strategic interests in the process. Although some of these potential opportunities have to do with how Africa interacts with its partners, a lot more will be dependent upon how Africa takes care of its own challenges and organises its own internal issues, particularly leveraging the opportunities that could be created through regional cooperation and integration. There are in this regard signs that the continent is waking up to the importance of its regional integration agenda, being determined to learn from the mistakes of the past and take advantage of opportunities that could come with the integration of the continent. Two noteworthy examples in this regard are the ongoing reform process of African Union institutions and the second being the creation of the African Continental Free Trade Area, with a secretariat in Accra, Ghana.

Talking about the importance of the CFTA, the 2017 Economic Commission for Africa (ECA) report on 'Assessing Regional Integration in Africa VIII' describe the CFTA as the flagship project of the African Union's Agenda 2063 and a key initiative that would boost the industrialisation and economic development of the continent. It argues that the CFTA has the potential to boost intra-African trade, stimulate investment and innovation, foster structural transformation, improve food security, enhance economic growth and export diversification, and rationalise the overlapping trade regimes of the main regional economic communities (RECs) (UNECA 2017: xi). According to the founding documents of the CFTA, the objectives of the CFTA include the creation of a single continental market for goods and services, with free movement of business persons and investments. This is undertaken with the aim of paving the way for accelerating the establishment of the Continental Customs Union and the African customs union. This will build into existing African Union programs on boosting intra-African trade through better harmonisation and coordination of trade liberalisation and facilitation regimes and instruments across RECs and across Africa in general. As part of these initiatives, these should hopefully resolve the challenges of multiple and overlapping memberships and enhance competitiveness at the industry and enterprise level by exploiting opportunities for scale production, continental market access and better reallocation of resources.

The CFTA is thus expected to amplify Africa's market and economic possibilities to the rest of the world and particularly to global investors and to promote the attainment of sustainable and inclusive socioeconomic development, and the structural transformation of the economies of the participating countries through the promotion of industrial development, that would result from and lead to the diversification of African economies regional value chain development, agricultural development and the eventual attainment of food security.

Again, the assumption in these expectations built into the CFTA hinges upon the hope that market integration shall deliver upon these promises once successfully accomplished. It is however worth mentioning that, whereas there are certainly some efficiency gains that could accrue to African economies with the elimination of certain barriers to trade and the promotion of intra-African trade, it may be overtly presumptuous to hope that the benefits of industrial development will accrue to the continent by mere market integration alone without deliberate coordination and promotion of a continental industrial policy, that clearly specifies the desired approach and pathway to its industrialisation and integration into the global economy and global production value chain. Without a commensurate emphasis on developing the continent's production capacities and technological capabilities, the establishment of the continental market under WTO rules of national treatment could only translate to the creation of a consumption hub for global production, where value is created and accumulated elsewhere, and consumption accentuated through the free movement of goods and persons on the continent. It is therefore imperative that an equal emphasis be placed on the continent's industrial and production capacity to accompany measures of the expansion of its markets.

With respect to the institutional reforms of the African Union, there are signs that the continent is undertaking steps to strengthen the functioning of the African Union and make it a more efficient organisation to drive the regional integration agenda. This is positive in the sense that it seeks to address some of the challenges highlighted in the earlier chapters of this book regarding the general challenges associated with regional integration on the continent. In a 2017 report titled 'The Imperative to Strengthen our Union', drafted under the annual AU presidency of President Kagame of Rwanda, it is argued that to strengthen the African Union, the following challenges need to be overcome:

i) The constant failure to see through African Union decisions which has resulted in a crisis of implementation.
ii) A limited relevance of the African Union to African citizens.
iii) A fragmented organisation with a multitude of focal areas.
iv) Overdependence on partner funding.
v) Underperformance of some organs and institutions due to unclear mandates or chronic underfunding.
vi) Limited managerial capacity.
vii) Lack of accountability for performance, at all levels.
viii) Unclear division of labour between the African Union Commission, the RECs, other regional mechanisms (RMs) and Member States.
ix) Inefficient working methods in both the Commission and the Assembly.

While this is probably not the first time such an initiative of this nature is undertaken, it is encouraging to recognise that the challenges are being acknowledged and steps undertaken to address the challenges faced by the

Union. There is an acknowledgement throughout the document of the importance of leadership and an appreciation of the following four actions that need to be undertaken to set things on the rail:

i) Focus on key priorities with continental scope.
ii) Realign African Union institutions to deliver against those priorities.
iii) Managing the African Union efficiently at both political and operational levels.
iv) Finance the African Union ourselves and sustainably.

The recommendations that are presented in this report for the future of the African Union are worthy of presentation without further analysis as they present the pathway that could ensure that the desired results are achieved. Accordingly, the report recommends:

i) The African Union should focus on a fewer number of priority areas that are by nature continental in scope, such as political affairs, peace and security, economic integration (including the CFTA) and Africa's global representation and voice.
ii) Accordingly, there should be a clear division of labour and effective collaboration between the African Union, RECs, RMs, Member States, and other continental institutions, in line with the principle of subsidiarity.

There are many more recommendations contained in that report than we have reported here but together they show a clear understanding and diagnostic of the challenges facing the African Union and its institutions. Although evaluation exercises of this nature are not new to the African Union, it is good and refreshing to note that there is a continued commitment towards improvement and to do better. There are enough resolutions of the African Union that have been taken and never implemented and as always the implementation challenge is one that needs to be overcome for meaningful change and progress to be registered. Hopefully, the momentum that is underway would lead to significant changes that would bring the AU to higher and superior levels of performance that make it ultimately set to accomplish its developmental mandate. The learning process associated with embarking upon reforms should hopefully generate enough spillover benefits and externalities that would extend into the other areas of the continent's agenda, including aspects of its industrialisation and development.

In contemplating the future of Africa and the implications of a successful approach to regionalism, we believe it is important to refocus attention on the question of Africa's industrialisation. Since history bears witness to the fact that the emergence of regions has been often associated with their growth in industrialisation, it seems reasonable to argue that Africa ought to follow the same pathway to emergence. For in reality, what other pathway to emergence could there exist if not the route of the continent's industrialisation? In this regard, the one thing that stands as an enormous source of inspiration that ought to guide the chosen course of action for Africa is the remarkable sustained growth in productivity and living standards that has characterised some of the East Asian economies in recent decades. One thing the Asian Miracle has done for Africa is to indicate to the continent that it is possible. Whereas underdeveloped countries are expected to take advantage of the innovation and technological advancements in other parts of the world, that has not been the case for Africa. It should be emphasised at this point of the conversation that herein lies the raison d' être , rationale and justification for a debate on developmental regionalism. The notion that there ought to be some positive externalities associated with pursuing developmental objectives within a regional integration agenda in a manner that will accrue benefits that may perhaps not have been possible to the participating countries unless they were involved in the regional integration project, or at least not to the scale made possible within the regional integration arrangement, to the extent that it makes the regional integration arrangement to have an additional appeal to participating members. This is one argument that has been made throughout this book, that there ought to be a justification and an argument made from a cost–benefit analysis perspective that encourages participating countries to want to be of a regional integration arrangement like the possibility of technology upgrading and what we can call 'collaborative industrialisation' that is mutually beneficial for participating countries.

To buttress this point, Justin Lin (2009) makes the argument that for a country to climb up the industrial and technological ladder, a host of other changes also need to take place: technologies need to become more complicated, capital requirements ought to increase, the scale of production ought to increase, the size of markets ought to increase to absorb the increased production and absorb the products (this includes domestic, regional and international markets, the whole essence of the export orientation argument – for a country cannot be export-oriented if it does not have goods to export for which there is a demand in the international markets). He also argues in this regard that market exchanges need to increasingly take place at arm's length, all of which led him to the conclusion that a flexible and smooth industrial and technological upgrading would require simultaneous improvements in education, financial and legal institutions as well as infrastructure that would facilitate both production and trade (Lin 2009: 485). Institutions alone would build efficiency into the systems, especially legal and financial institutions but they ought to be at best only accompanying measures to the technology upgrade, production upgrade and expansion in markets. Whereas together they make up an inclusive combination of important factors, it is surely possible to make the argument regarding the order in which they ought to be accumulated in any single country and much more on how their acquisition can be pursued as a regional project.

Looking at all these factors, the one ingredient that seems evidently prioritised in the African integration project is the market access question which has recently been enhanced with the conversations around the creation of the African Continental Free Trade Area. Once treated as part of a comprehensive regional integration project, it ought to solve the market access component of the equation by creating a larger market for African products, accompanied by increased factor mobility. However, market access alone and larger markets would not automatically translate to technological upgrading or more sophisticated production that could amount to the collective pursuit of industrialisation objectives. Suggesting in the process that some more deliberate actions ought to accompany Africa's regional integration projects that focus on technology upgrading, production expansion and the development of requisite institutions (legal and financial) to accompany a possible continental industrialisation agenda.

CONCLUSION

It should come as no surprise that this volume should close by raising more questions than some of the propositions that it has argued for in the last couple of chapters. This approach intends to buttress the notion that as far as it concerns the issues of Africa's development, there are more questions than answers given the complexity of the continent's history and the enormity of its contemporary challenges. However, the fundamental motivation of this volume has not just been about the most suitable ways of promoting regional integration on the continent but has someone been on how the objectives of integration and development could be jointly pursued as part of the continent's regional integration agenda, within a paradigm taunted as developmental regionalism. Far from being an innovative concept having been explored by other authors in the past, its emphasis in this volume has been motivated by the desire to make the case that embracing developmental regionalism would entail approaching and conducting the regional integration agenda differently. Seen from this perspective, the reason this volume ends with more questions than answers is because it does not interrogate sufficiently some of the fundamental assumptions built into both the promises of regional integration and the practice of development on the continent, some of the neoliberal orthodoxies assumed into the benefits of linear market integration and the many promised benefits that have not accrued from mere trade liberalisation alone on the continent. The one message this message has wanted to drive across is the argument that development should be pursued alongside the integration agenda and that this would require doing integration differently and approaching the agenda with more developmental focus, as opposed to assuming that certain developmental benefits do accrue as the natural outcomes of integration, including market integration. The latter argument merits further interrogation in the context of Africa and urgently so given the fact that the pursuit of market integration is a corner objective of African regionalism as evidenced through the objectives built into the Abuja Treaty and now the new emphasis on the African Continental Free Trade Area. In our sense, the promised and expected developmental benefits have not been sufficiently interrogated and merit to do so. This is important so that all effort is not merely invested in trying to eliminate trade barriers and promote market integration, whereas market integration in itself may hold only a limited promise of the elimination of certain inefficiencies that would better allocate existing resources, but doesn't get into questions of upgrading existing endowments or restructuring the economies to take advantage. This leads to the second core but the less emphasised message of this volume which also merits a more detailed investigation, that is the argument around industrialisation and Africa's path to industrialisation as a source of its growth and prosperity and how best this can and should also be pursued within a developmental regionalism paradigm.

However, as Ankomah (2015) has argued, history has repeatedly shown that the single most important thing that distinguishes rich countries from poor ones is basically their higher capabilities in manufacturing where productivity is generally higher, and more importantly, where this productivity tends to grow faster than in agriculture or services. Chang (2009) has argued in this regard that the very thing that makes countries developed or not is their differential abilities to develop and use technologies, also known as their 'technological capabilities'. He argues in this regard that rich countries are rich and poor countries poor because the former can use, and develop, technologies that the latter cannot use, let alone develop (Chang 2009: 490). He further argues that the process of acquiring higher technological capabilities is such that a country trying to catch up with a more technologically advanced country needs to set up and protect industries in which it does not have a comparative advantage because the lagging country cannot wait until it accumulates enough physical and human capital before it enters a more advanced industry that uses physical and human capital more intensely. While this falls within the ongoing debates on possible pathways to industrialisation, the role of manufacturing and the traditional responsibility of governments to promote industrialisation (viz the comparative advantage approach a la Justin Lin versus created competitive advantage through the alternation of initial factor endowments), the salient argument of this volume is that the question of Africa's industrialisation needs to be revisited. It has been argued thus far that this revisitation should happen within a developmental regionalism paradigm that centre stages a joint industrial policy as a corner piece of the regional integration agenda. What format this needs to take and what adjustments ought to be made to ongoing debates about industrialisation is worthy of further research and interrogation. There is an obvious bias here for the historicity of manufacturing-led industrialisation in lifting the community of nations out of underdevelopment to a pathway of prosperity, interpreted together with the role that deliberate and strategic policy approaches and options have played in facilitating these transformational processes. Strategic policy options here is referring to the requisite flexibility to judge context and theory together in making choices that produce the desired results being sought by policy proponents. As Ha Joon Chang (2008) in an interview in *Multinational Monitor* on his book (*Bad Samaritans*) argues, the manufacturing sector has empirically (over the years and in the experience of several developed countries) been the sector that has shown the highest productivity, the fastest rate of technological progress and productivity growth with the biggest spillover impact into other sectors, which provides grounds for the future of developing countries (including African countries) to seem promising/bright in manufacturing.

Bibliography

Adedeji, A. (2002) "From the Lagos Plan of Action to the New Partnership for African Development, and from the Final Act of Lagos to the Constitutive Act: Whither Africa?" *Keynote address at the African Forum for Envisioning Africa. Nairobi, Kenya.* 26–29 April.

Acharya, A. (2009) *Whose Ideas Matter: Agency and Power in Asian Regionalism* (Ithaca and London: Cornell University Press).

Acharya, A. and Johnston, A. (eds.) (2007) *Crafting Cooperation: Regional International Institutions in Comparative Perspective* (Cambridge, MA: Cambridge University Press).

Adejumobi, S. and Kreiter, Z. (2016) "The Theory and Discourse of Developmental Regionalism." Paper presented Regional Forum on: Developmental Regionalism, Peace and Economic Transformation in Southern Africa, organised by the ECA from 28–30 September 2016. Africa Review 15.

Akokpari, J. (2008) "Dilemmas of Regional Integration and Development in Africa." In *The African Union and its Institutions*, edited by J. Akokpari, A. Ndinga-Muvumba, and T. Murithi, 85–110 (Johannesburg: Fanele Publishers).

Asante, S. K. B. (1997) *Regionalism and Africa's Development: Expectations, Reality and Challenges* (London: Macmillan Press Ltd.).

Axline, W. A. (ed.) (1994) *The Political Economy of Regional Cooperation: Comparative Case Studies* (London: Pinter).

Bach, D. (1999) "Regionalism in Africa: Concepts and Contexts." In *Regionalisation in Africa: Integration and Disintegration* (Suffolk, UK: James Currey Publishers).

Bach, D. (2008) "The AU and the EU." In *The African Union and Its Institutions*, edited by J. Akokpari, A. Ndinga-Muvumba, and T. Murithi, 355–381 (Johannesburg: Fanele Publishers).

Bach, D. (2013) "Thick Institutionalism versus Lean Integration: New Regionalism in Africa." In *Regional Integration and Social Cohesion*, edited by Candice Moore, 93–106 (Pieterlen and Bern, Switzerland: P. L. E. Peter Lang).

Balassa, B. (1961) *The Theory of Economic Integration* (Homewood, Illinois: R. D. Irwin).

Brenton, P. and Hoffman, B. (2016) *Political Economy of Regional Integration in Sub-Saharan Africa*. Washington, DC: World Bank. https://openknowledge.worldbank.org/handle/10986/24767. License: CC BY 3.0IGO.

Davies, R. (1996) "Promoting Regional Integration in Africa: An Analysis of Prospects and Problems from a South African Perspective." *African Security Review* 5(5): 27–38. doi:10.1080/10246029.1996.9627823.

Dinka, T. and Kennes, W. (2007) "Africa's Regional Integration Arrangements: History and Challenges." ECDPM Discussion Article No. 74, September.

Dolowitz, D. P. and Marsh, D. (2000) "Learning from Abroad: The Role of Policy Transfer in Contemporary Policy Making." *Governance: An International Journal of Policy and Administration* 13(1): 5–24.

Draper, P. (2010) "Rethinking the (European) Foundations of Sub-Saharan African Regional Economic Integration: A Political Economy Essay." OECD Development Centre Working Papers, No. 293. Paris: OECD Publishing. doi:10.1787/5km5zrs9075k-en.

Draper, P. (2012) "Breaking Free from Europe: Why African Needs Another Model of Integration." In *Regionalism in a Changing World: Comparative Perspectives in the New Global Order*, edited by L. Fioramonti (London: Routledge).

Eder, J. (2021) "Moving Towards Developmental Regionalism? Industrial Cooperation in the Eurasian Economic Union from an Armenian and Belarusian Perspective." *Post-Communist Economies* 33(2–3): 331–358. doi:10.1080/14631377.2020.1793590.

European Commission. (1995) European Community Support for Regional Integration Efforts among Developing Countries. Communication from the Commission, 16 June. Brussels.

European Commission. (2005) EU Strategy for Africa: Towards a Euro-African Pact to Accelerate Africa's Development. Communication from the Parliament and Council. http://eurlex.europa.eu/LexUriServ/LexUriServ.do?uri=COM:2005:0489:FIN:EN:PDF.

Fioramonti, L. (2013) "The Bumper Sticker: Why Africa Is Not Following the European Model of Integration." Paper presented at the International Studies Association Annual Convention, San Francisco, 2–7 April.

Geda, A. and Kibret, H. (2007) "Regional Economic Integration in Africa: A Review of Problems and Prospects with a Case Study of COMESA." *Journal of African Economies* 17(3): 357–394.

Haastrup, T. (2013) "EU as Mentor? Promoting Regionalism as External Relations Practice in EU–Africa Relations." *Journal of European Integration* 35(7): 785–800.

Ismail, F. (2019) "A Developmental Regionalism Approach to the African Continental Free Trade Area (AfCTA)." *Journal of Reviews on Global Economics* 8: 1771–1785.

Jetschke, A. (2010) "Do Regional Organizations Travel? European Integration, Diffusion and the Case of ASEAN." The Transformative Power of Europe (KFG).

Jetschke, A. and Murray, P. (2012) "Diffusing Regional Integration: The EU and South East Asia." *Western European Politics* 35(1): 174–191.

Jetschke, A. and Lenz, T. (2012) "Does Regionalism Diffuse? A New Research Agenda for the Study of Regional Organizations." *Journal of European Public Policy* 20(4): 626–637.

Joint Africa-EU Strategy (JAES). (2007) The Africa-EU Strategic Partnership a Joint Africa-EU Strategy. http://www.africa-eu-artnership.org/sites/default/files /documents/eas2007_joint_strategy_en.pdf.

Kaplinsky, R. and Morris, M. (2001) A Handbook for Value Chain Research. Institute of Development Studies, Univeristy of Sussex, Brighton, UK.

Lenz, T. (2012) "Spurred Emulation: The EU and Regional Integration in Mercosur and SADC." *West European Politics* 35(1): 155–173. https://doi.org/10.1080/014 02382.2012.631319.

Marsh, D. and Sharman, J.C. (2009) "Policy Diffusion and Policy Transfer." *Policy Studies* 80(3): 269–288.

Mattli, W. (1999) *The Logic of Regional Integration – Europe and Beyond* (Cambridge: Cambridge University Press).

McCarthy, C. (1999) "Regional Integration in Sub-Saharan Africa: Past, Present and Future." In *Regional Integration and Trade Liberalization in Sub Saharan Africa, Volume 4, Synthesis and Review*, edited by A. Oyejide, B. Ndulu, and D. Greenaway (London: Macmillan Press Ltd).

Meseguer, C. and Gilardi, F. (2009) "What Is New in the Study of Policy Diffusion?" *Review of International Political Economy* 16(3): 527–543.

Mevel, S. and Karingi, S. (2013) "Towards a Continental Free Trade Area in Africa: A CGE Modelling Assessment with a Focus on Agriculture." In *Shared Harvests: Agriculture, Trade, and Employment*, edited by D. Cheong, M. Jansen, and R. Peters. International Labour Office and United Nations Conference on Trade and Development.

Motsamai, D. and Qobo, M. (2012) "Regionalism in Africa: Development Crises and the Growing Influence of Emerging Powers." In *Regions and Crises*, edited by L. Fioramonti, 145–162 (London: Palgrave Macmillan).

Moravcsik, A. (1993) "Preferences and Power in the European Community: A Liberal Intergovernmentalist Approach." *Journal of Common Market Studies* 31(4): 473–524.

Morris, M. and Fessehaie, J. (2014) "The Industrialisation Challenge for Africa: Towards a Commodities Based Industrialisation Path." *Journal of African Trade* 1(1): 25–36.

Mukamunana, R. and Moeti, K. (2005) "Challenges of Regional Integration in Africa: Policy and Administrative Implications." *Journal of Public Administration*, Conference Proceedings, pp. 90101, 1 Oct. https://hdl.handle.net/10520/EJC51225

Myers, D. J. (2000) "The Diffusion of Collective Violence: Infectiousness, Susceptibility, and Mass Media Networks." *American Journal of Sociology* 106(1): 173–208.

Nkrumah, K. (1963) *Africa Must Unite* (New York: Frederick A. Praeger).

Nye, J. (1965) *Pan-Africanism and the East African Integration* (Cambridge: Cambridge University Press).

Nyerere, J. (2006 [1997]) "Without Unity, There Is No Future for Africa." *New African*, 20–23 February.

Olivier, G. (2010) "Regionalism in Africa: Cooperation Without Integration?" *Strategic Review of Southern Africa* 32(2): 17–43.

Oyejide, A., Ndulu, B. and Greenaway, D. (1999) *Regional Integration and Trade Liberalization in Sub Saharan Africa, Volume 4, Synthesis and Review* (London: Macmillan Press Ltd.).

Qobo, M. (2007) "The Challenges of Regional Integration in Africa: In the Context of Globalisation and the Prospects for a United States of Africa." ISS Paper 145, June.

Richard, R. (1991) "What Is Lesson Drawing?" *Journal of Public Policy* 11: 3–30.

Shaw, T., Soderbaum, F., Nyang'oro, J. E. and Grant, J. A. (2005) "The Future of Regionalism in Africa." In *The New Regionalism in Africa*, edited by J. A. Grant and F. Soderbaum (Aldershot: Ashgate).

Sloan, J. W. (1971) "The Strategy Of Developmental Regionalism: Benefits, Distribution, Obstacles, and Capabilities." *Journal of Common Market Studies* 10(2): 138–162.

Strang, D. and Meyer, J. W. (1993) "Institutional Conditions for Diffusion." *Theory & Society* 22: 487–512.

United Nations Economic Commission for Africa – UNECA. (2006) *Assessing Regional Integration in Africa II: Rationalizing Regional Economic Communities* (Addis Ababa: UNECA and African Union). http://www.uneca.org/aria.

United Nations Economic Commission for Africa – UNECA. (2008) *Assessing Regional Integration in Africa 2008: Towards Monetary and Financial Integration in Africa* (Addis Ababa: UNECA). http://www.uneca.org/aria.

United Nations Economic Commission for Africa – UNECA. (2010) *Economic Report on Africa, 2010* (Addis Ababa: UNECA).

Vanheukelom, J. and Bertelsmann-Scott, T. (2016) "The Political Economy of Regional Integration in Africa: The Southern African Development Community (SADC) Report." https://ecdpm.org/work/the-political-economy-of-regional-integration-in-africa-the-southern-african-development-community-sadc.

Viner, J. (1950) *The Customs Union Issue* (New York: Carnegie Endowment for International Peace).

Viner, J. (1958) "Stability and Progress: The Poorer Countries' Problem." In *Stability and Progress in the World Economy*, edited by D. Hague, 41–65 (London: Palgrave Macmillan).

Index

About the Author

Dr Gabila Fohtung Nubong is a political economist with a master's in economics and PhD in international relations from the University of Pretoria (UP). He is currently an associate professor at the School of Economics, North-West University, South Africa. His research interests are principally in comparative regionalism with a focus on European Union and African Union integration processes. He also has a keen interest in African growth and economic development questions and his recent research has focused on institutions, foreign direct investment and regional economic integration. He has worked as an economist for the European Union Delegation to South Africa and as a project officer at the European Centre for Development Policy Management (ECDPM) in Maastricht, The Netherlands. He was a postdoctoral fellow at the Institute for Strategic Policy Analysis (ISPA) at UP and a research fellow at the Centre for Governance Innovation at UP.